# BOOMERANG

## How to Throw, Catch, and Make It.

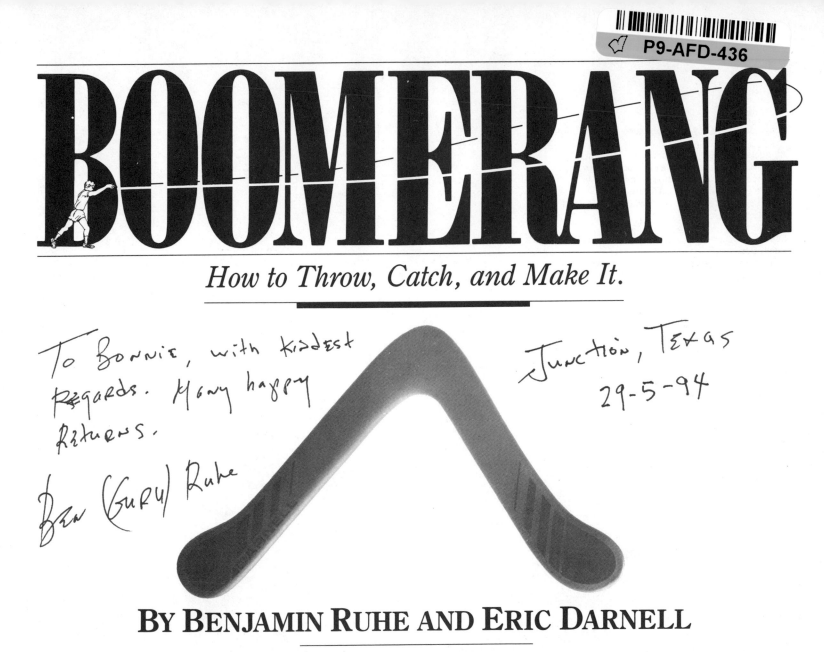

To Bonnie, with kindest
Regards. Many happy
Returns.

Ben (GURU) Ruhe

Junction, Texas
29-5-94

## BY BENJAMIN RUHE AND ERIC DARNELL

### ILLUSTRATIONS BY CHESLYE LARSON

Workman Publishing, New York

Library of Congress Cataloging in Publication Data
Ruhe, Benjamin.
    Boomerang: how to throw, catch, and make it.

    Bibliography: p.
    1. Boomerangs.   I. Darnell, Eric.   II. Title.
GV1097.B65R84   1985        796.4'35
85-40523
ISBN 0-89480-935-0
Book and cover design: Tedd Arnold
Cover illustration: Cheslye Larson
Front cover photographs: Chuck Carlton (top);
George Leavens (middle); Holly English Payne
(bottom). Back cover: Holly English Payne (right).

Workman Publishing
1 West 39 Street
New York, NY 10018

Manufactured in the United States of America
First Printing September 1985
10 9 8 7 6 5 4 3 2 1

**Additional Darnell boomer-
angs are available through
Turning Point, Inc., South
Strafford, Vermont 05070.**

# WARNING

Do not use boomerangs until you have learned the safety rules on page 20 of this book. Always follow the safety rules. Boomerangs are sporting articles, not children's toys. The publisher and its distributors shall have no liability for use of the boomerang supplied with this book or for use of any other boomerang.

A right-handed boomerang comes with this book. Left-handers, turn to page 33 for special throwing instructions.

# CONTENTS

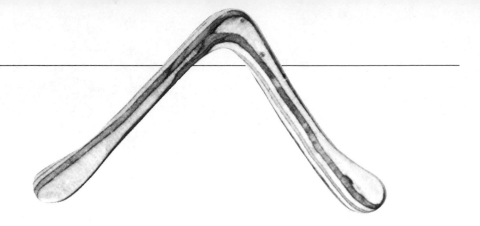

# GAMES AND COMPETITIONS

# WELCOME TO BOOMERANGING

BOOMERANG THROWING IS A minor miracle, endlessly repeated. You throw a curved stick of wood away from you as hard as you can. It spins outward, tests the breeze, curves and climbs—and obediently comes winging home, whispering as it flies close and hovers softly down to your hands.

You experience the same delight that the boomerang's Australian Aboriginal creators felt ten thousand years ago. In tune with your surroundings, you sense the shifts in the wind; you learn the personality of each boomerang you throw and how much space it needs to fly. You are smitten with the expansive feeling of sending yourself through the air. There are no gimmicks: what you put into your throw is what you get back.

If you make your own boomerang, the alchemy of creating a design, carving the shape and smoothing the airfoils harks back to an age-old toolmaking ritual that curiously satisfies a deep-down instinct. In no other sport do you have so much input into your equipment. You don't tune your golf clubs or carve your own baseball bat, but in boomeranging you can choose between plywood and polypropylene, styrofoam or natural wood elbows; you can throw two-, three-, four-, five- or six-armed varieties, and you can tune the wings every which way and still call what you're using a boomerang.

The sophisticated aerodynamics of the boomerang continue to captivate physicists and aerospace engineers, yet it couldn't be simpler to throw and catch. In the 1980s we have the Space Age rocket that follows a simple parabolic curve: launched here, it lands there. The boomerang is more complex: launched here, it lands here. It provides its own lift and uses its special shape to change direction. It actually flies.

Part mystery, part science, mildly eccentric and very good exercise, the boomerang matches the temper of our time. This book is a way of sharing our passion for the magic stick that has taken over our lives. We wish to thank Workman editor Susan Gough Henly, copy editor Lynn Strong, designer Tedd Arnold and photographer Holly English Payne for helping to make it possible.

66 In the early days of the Dreamtime, people had to crawl on their hands and knees because the sky was nearly touching the ground. An old chief came to a magic pool and he stooped down to drink. As he did so, he saw a beautiful straight stick in the water and he reached in and picked it up. Then he suddenly thought, 'I can push up the sky with this stick and we'll be able to stand up.' So he pushed and pushed until he pushed the sky to where it is today and the trees began to grow and the possums ran about in the branches and the kangaroos started hopping for joy. Then he looked at his stick and saw it was terribly bent. Thinking it was no longer good, he threw it away but it came back to him. He tried again and it came back again. So he kept the stick and called it the boomerang. 99

—*Australian Aboriginal legend as told by Les and Arthur Janetski*

# HOW IT ALL STARTED

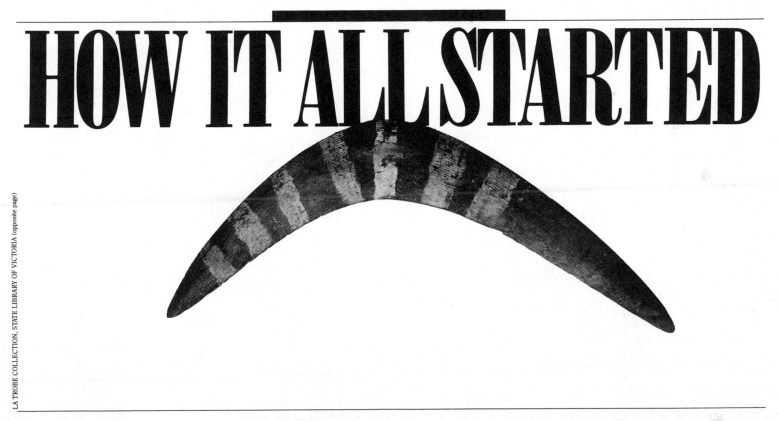

THE MAGICAL BOOMERANG, A source of wonder even to today's Space Age scientists, dates all the way back to the primitive Aborigines who roamed the continent of Australia long before the dawn of civilization. We know this because a recent discovery of boomerangs, in a peat bog southwest of Adelaide, led to carbon-14 tests that pegged their age at between 11 and 15 thousand years. But how did a prehistoric culture, with no more at its disposal than the simplest tools, transform a stick of wood into a sophisticated device that could fly like a bird and return unerringly to the hand that launched it?

## THE KILLER-STICK

Roaming hundreds of miles on their "walkabouts" through a vast, mostly desert landscape, the Aborigines eked out a meager existence by foraging and hunting for food. Game was brought down by throwing rocks, boulders and tree limbs, which allowed the hunters to keep out of harm's way. Eventually the wooden club evolved, and this

*Equipped for the hunt, an Aborigine prepares to launch his "throwstick" with a vengeance.*

weapon apparently developed into the "killer-stick"—a thinned-down, banana-shaped missile that cut a deadly three-foot-wide swath through the air as it spun at lightning speed. Thrown sidearm, the killer-stick sailed long and straight, its curve stabilizing and lengthening its flight, its slim lines creating the beginnings of a convex shape to generate lift in the manner of a bird's wing.

The killer-stick could *fly*. In fact, it possessed all the essential elements that, slightly modified and refined, almost certainly led to the boomerang. Imagine an Aborigine at work one day on his killer-stick, honing it down to fashion an even lighter weapon. Perhaps he experiments with the curve, or perhaps a sharper curve was produced naturally by an unusual twisting of the green wood as it dried. And just perhaps, upon observing more closely the shape of a bird's wing, he refines the convex shape so that each of the wings is flat on bottom and rounded on top.

Now picture the hunter standing downwind from his prey, spinning his killer-stick through the air, and to his amazement the new-shaped weapon, partly blown by the wind, curves sharply around and starts back toward him! Surely this will lead to further

**FICTION:** Boomerangs were used by the Aborigines to kill kangaroos and other big game.

*GARY LARSON, CHRONICLE FEATURES, 1984*

**FACT:** A close relative of the boomerang, the non-returning killer-stick, was the device used for hunting large animals. The smaller, lighter and aerodynamically different returning boomerang was used in sport and ritual. Its hunting function was limited to knocking down birds.

SMITHSONIAN INSTITUTION

CHUCK CARLTON

*Three killer-sticks and a returning boomerang (third from top). Note the boomerang's sharper curve, forming two distinct wings.*

# KILLER-STICKS AROUND THE WORLD

The killer-stick was used widely not only in Australia but also in many other areas throughout the world. Undoubtedly replaced in some regions by the more efficient bow and arrow, it hung on in the places where it worked best: semi-arid plains with few trees or bushes to impede flight. Killer-sticks have been found in ancient Egypt, southern India, North Africa, northern Europe, and North and South America. The Hopi and other Indians of the American Southwest use their version for hunting rabbits. These rabbit sticks are of ancient origin: the Anasazi, the Hopis' pre-Columbian ancestors, also used them.

Some of the most fascinating killer-sticks outside Australia have been uncovered by Egyptologists. English archaeologist Howard Carter, whose discovery of Tutankhamen's tomb startled the world in the 1920s, has published photographs of the killer-sticks found on the site.

*A Hopi Indian hunter brings home his prize.*

experiments as other hunters join in the fun, trying out different designs and launch angles, and ultimately learning how to use the wind to their advantage. We can surmise that they discovered a vertical launch gave them consistently returning flight patterns and, in this way, an entirely new type of "throw-stick" evolved.

Our scenario is purely speculative, of course, yet most authorities agree that the boomerang is indeed an offshoot of the hunter's killer-stick.

# THE BOOMERANG

While the killer-stick was found over large areas of the Australian continent, the boomerang was much less common. It's unique, elliptical flight path gives us a hint of the very different role it played in the Aboriginal culture. Unlike the killer-stick, the boomerang was used primarily for sport and bird hunting.

## SPORT

Early explorers reported competitions to determine which man could throw a boomerang in the greatest number of circles before it returned to a peg in the ground. One nineteenth-century account describes a curious game in which half a dozen Aborigines stood in file, each resting his hands on the shoulders of the man in front, while a thrower positioned himself some distance away and tossed a boomerang over their heads. As it circled around and swooped down, everyone in the file tried to dodge out of its way—with those who were unsuccessful being struck a painful blow. Each man got a chance to throw, and the man who hit the most people was the winner.

Another report describes a primitive fireworks display in Queensland, where boomerangs lit with live coals were hurled aloft to spin through the night sky.

## HUNTING BIRDS

Since a boomerang flies too high to be thrown at game animals and is too small and light to do much damage to a big kangaroo or emu, its use in hunting was apparently restricted to wildfowl. It was very effective when hurled into a dense flock of ducks, geese or swans, knocking two or three fowl out of the sky in one throw. As an added bonus, if it missed entirely, the boomerang came flying back to the hunter for another try.

A second hunting use involved nets made of plant-root fiber and hung across narrow stretches of water or over flyways between lakes. When a flight of water birds was sighted, hunters would imitate the cry of a hawk and throw boomerangs high into

*Aborigines approach their quarry, using clumps of grass as cover.*

# THE MAGIC MISSILE

The accounts of boomerangs by early white explorers and settlers in Australia were highly exaggerated. One observer claimed the boomerang "disappeared" from sight for several minutes before returning to the thrower. Fifty years after Captain Cook's first landing on the continent, others were still claiming that the objects were wooden swords.

CULVER PICTURES

The explorer Major Thomas Mitchell gave this part observant, part fanciful account of the *bommereng* in his *Three Expeditions into the Interior of Eastern Australia,* published in London in 1839:

"The *bommereng,* a thin curved missile, can be thrown by a skillful hand, so as to rise upon the air, and thus to deviate from the ordinary path of projectiles, its crooked course being, nevertheless, equally under control. It is about two feet four inches long and is cut, according to the grain, from the curved parts of acacia or other standing trees of compact hardwood. They usually weigh about 9½ ounces. One side, which is the uppermost in throwing, is slightly convex, and is sometimes elaborately carved. The lower side is flat, and plain. The bommereng is held, not as a sabre, but sickle-wise, or concave towards the thrower; and, as a rotatory motion is imparted to it when sent off, the air presents so much resistance to the flat side, and so little to the sharp edge as it cuts forward, that the long sustained flight of the whirling missile seems independent of the common effect of gravitation.

"The native, from long practice, can do astonishing things with this weapon. He seems to determine, with great certainty, what its crooked and distant flight shall be, and how and where it is to end. Thus he frequently amuses himself in hurling the formidable weapon to astonishing heights and distances, from one spot to which the missile returns, to fall beside him.

"The contrivance probably originated in the utility of such a missile for the purpose of killing ducks where they are very numerous, as on the interior rivers and lagoons, and where, accordingly, we find it much more in use than on the sea-coast, and better made, being often covered with good carving."

the air to simulate birds of prey. Alarmed, the birds would fly low, right into the nets, where waiting women and children pulled the traps shut.

## RITUALS

As in all implement-poor cultures, the tools used by the Aborigines were included in their rituals. Thus boomerangs and killer-sticks became musical instruments when twirled around in the air, thumped percussively on the ground or clacked together with a second stick. Used as bows, they were rubbed across the edge of another boomerang to make a curious musical sound. In Cairns, Queensland, members of the Kunggandyi tribe twirled an unusual cross-stick boomerang, the *pirbu pirbu*, in a rhythmic accompaniment as dancers shuffled in a circle.

## OTHER FUNCTIONS

Archaeologists have also surmised that both killer-sticks and boomerangs were used to dig for water and clear

HEINEMANN PUBLISHERS AUSTRALIA PTY LTD.

*Boomerangs become "clapping-sticks" when used to accompany dancers at a corroboree.*

## "EVOCATIVE GLOTTAL GURGLES"

One of the reasons there have been so many misconceptions about the function of the boomerang is that the early colonists applied the word *bumerang*, which they took from the now-vanished Tharawal and Daruk tribes of New South Wales, to both the returning and non-returning throw-sticks. Both devices, the true boomerang and the killer-stick, still carry the "boomerang" designation and this has caused confusion about what each does and how it looks.

Within the Aboriginal culture they were known by more than 300 names, from *ullagunga* to *warrayagga*, *munkarara* to *baranganj*—"all evocative glottal gurgles," an English humorist has remarked. Evocative of what? "Possibly of the noise you make when they come back unexpectedly and hit you in the throat," he suggests.

Other titles include:

| | |
|---|---|
| *Tootgundy* | *Duludurili* |
| *Kadimaka* | *Parabawitua* |
| *Nanjal* | *Ketketum* |
| *Barngeet* | *Ileila* |
| *Kilie* | *Aribina* |
| *Jalkabari* | *Tutukera* |
| *Gatingatin* | *Warazaing* |

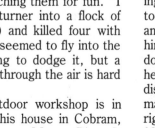

# JACKIE BYHAM

## *The Walkabout Man*

SCANCOLOR. MOORABBIN, AUSTRALIA

Jackie Byham crafted his first boomerang at age 13—"It nearly took the head off the poor bloody postman on his push bike," he recalls—and has been making and throwing them ever since.

A commando during World War II and a surveyor after the war, Byham decided to sell some boomerangs at the 1956 Olympic Games in Melbourne. He turned out five thousand big, heavy plywood copies of Aboriginal models and "sold the whole damn lot." This launched him into boomerang-making as a full-time profession.

A man prone to modern-day "walkabouts," Byham has explored much of the Australian continent by truck in search of Aboriginal lore and objects. He has documented the use of killer-sticks by Aborigines in hunting rabbits and other small game and has himself hunted with boomerangs in addition to throwing and catching them for fun. "I once threw a returner into a flock of galas (cockatoos) and killed four with one throw. They seemed to fly into the boomerang, trying to dodge it, but a stick that curves through the air is hard to avoid."

Byham's outdoor workshop is in the backyard of his house in Cobram, Victoria, on the upper Murray River. It is flanked on one side by cages of colorful cockatoos, parrots and cockateels, and on the other by a field housing his pet emus and kangaroos. Also in his backyard is a small log cabin museum that displays his finest artifacts, including bark paintings, ceremonial items, tools, weapons and, of course, boomerangs. His most prized returner came to him quite unexpectedly: while chopping down an old dead eucalyptus tree, he heard a thud in a patch of leaves and discovered an Aboriginal boomerang made with stone tools. Since the Aborigines left the Murray River area in the 1850s, the boomerang is at least 130 years old, but it may well be a lot older than that. Nearby, archaeologists have found the remains of the earliest man known on the continent, his age having been estimated at over 40 thousand years.

Now, after years of grappling with sawdust and chain smoking ("I like to cough, that's why I smoke," he says), Byham has retired from his Binghi Boomerangs business. His nephew, Peter Byham, continues the tradition, however, and is now turning out some of the finest competition boomerangs seen Down Under. No one is prouder of him than Jackie Byham.

fire sites, to unearth honey ants and lizards, to scrape hot ashes from baked animals and to sharpen flint tools by striking flakes from them. Used as a friction saw on softwood, the boomerang created sparks that were caught in tinder to make fire. Its functions extended to the ridiculous: an Aborigine was once seen using a boomerang to clean his teeth.

# SUMMING UP

Distinguishing between the killer-stick and the boomerang can be a confusing task. Dr. Norman Tindale, former anthropologist at the South Australian Museum in Adelaide, reports seeing Aborigines taking a boomerang and twisting it over a fire to convert it into a non-returning killer-stick for the day's hunting. The wooden implement later could be retwisted to become a returning boomerang.

Thus the boomerang could be a hunting device one day, an object for sport another, a ceremonial implement the third. Meanwhile, it served as a cleaver or lever used in digging, knapping flint and making fire.

HEINEMANN PUBLISHERS AUSTRALIA PTY LTD.

*Boomerangs played an integral role in the daily life of Aboriginal tribes.*

**❝**Of all the advantages we have derived from our Australian settlements, none seems to have given more universal satisfaction than the introduction of some crooked pieces of wood shaped like the crescent moon, and called boomerang, or kilee. Ever since their structure has been fully understood, carpenters appear to have ceased from all other work; the windows of toy shops exhibit little else; walking sticks and umbrellas have gone out of fashion; and even in this rainy season no man carries anything but a boomerang; nor does this species of madness appear to be abating.**❞**
—DUBLIN UNIVERSITY MAGAZINE,
*February 1838*

> **"**The boomerang is a wonderful invention that starts out in one spot, faithfully returns, and makes a lovely flight of fancy in between. It's hard not to admire a piece of wood that can find its own way home.**"**
> —*Steve Hall, New York-based free-lance writer*

# THROWING FOR GOOD RETURNS

# SAFETY RULES

READ THESE RULES CARE-FULLY BEFORE YOU BEGIN TO THROW YOUR BOOMERANG. Remember that it can be very hard to predict where a boomerang will land, especially for beginners and for anyone throwing under windy conditions. A clear understanding of the following rules will keep boomeranging a safe sport for all concerned.

## BASIC SAFETY RULES

**1** The playing field should be a large, flat, grassy area, free of holes and obstructions such as rocks and trees, with a hundred yards of clear space in *all* directions from the thrower. Spectators must be kept well away from the perimeter of the playing area. For this reason, beaches, parks and other locales that tend to attract crowds are unsuitable for throwing boomerangs. Young children should never be permitted on the playing field.

**2** Boomerangs should be brightly colored and/or decorated for high visibility. Edges should be rounded, not sharp or rough, to ensure safe catches. Plywood boomerangs that are cracked or otherwise in need of repair can splinter in the hand and should therefore be left at home.

**3** Throwing should take place only in calm weather conditions. The boomerang's flight path cannot be controlled when the wind is blowing more than 12 mph.

**4** Beginners should use lightweight boomerangs exclusively until they have mastered the basic principles of throwing and catching. It is also helpful for beginners to wear long-sleeved shirts, gloves and/or wristbands to protect their hands and arms from possible bruises.

## THROWING RULES

**1** Before the first throw, and before each throw thereafter, check to see that no one has moved into the playing area. If more than one thrower is on the field, a central launching point should be established with each thrower taking turns. Do not permit any wandering around the field while boomerangs are in the air.

**2** Always throw at a 50° angle to the wind (to the right if you are throwing a right-handed boomerang and to the left if you are throwing a left-handed one). Boomerangs thrown downwind or too much into the wind will not return.

**3** *Never* throw sidearm or underarm. A boomerang launched with too much "layover" soars upward, stalls, then zooms down for a crash-landing. Do not attempt to catch a boomerang that comes in fast or pendulums down at a sharp angle. Keep it in view, but step aside to avoid it as it lands.

**4** Remember that a boomerang can cause injury, especially if it hits the face or a part of the body where the bone is very close to the skin. Watch your boomerang during its entire flight.

If it is returning wildly and looks like it might hit you, step aside, turn your back, duck, and cover your head. If you see that it is veering toward someone else on the field, shout a warning so that he can protect himself. Throwers are rarely hit by their own boomerangs (because they are watching them closely). Always keep an eye out for *other people's* boomerangs and wait until everyone has thrown before retrieving your own.

**5** Never let others fly your boomerang unless they have been properly instructed. Novice throwers should always be supervised. Damage to people and property can result if a friend decides to give your boomerang a trial heave without prior instruction.

**6** Never toss a boomerang to someone. Walk over and hand it to him.

**7** Wear sunglasses when throwing in bright conditions. Unbreakable plastic safety sunglasses are recommended both as facial protection and for added visibility if necessary.

**8** Be courteous at all times and, above all, exercise common sense.

W ITH A GOOD BOOMER-ang and a little finesse, you'll be throwing with precision in no time at all. Launched with sufficient spin and proper follow-through, your boomerang will not only return but fly circles around you before it hovers down to your outstretched hands.

Novices tend to be a little overawed at the thought of boomerang-ing, perhaps because they feel there must be some trick that gives the 'rang its seemingly magi-cal flight pattern. Quite the contrary. Throw-ing a boomerang so that it returns to you is as simple as throwing a baseball. In fact, the action is identical; the only difference is that the wind must be taken into account.

Basically you follow five steps in the throw itself:

∧ Position yourself at a 50° angle to the right of the wind (to the left of the wind if you're throwing a left-handed boomerang).

∧ Grip either wingtip firmly with the flat side of the boomerang in your palm.

∧ Hold the boomer-ang vertically (never sidearm).

∧ Aim at distant tree or house tops.

∧ Cock the boomerang back over your shoulder, take a step forward and re-lease with a whip-cracking mo-tion to impart momentum and the all-important spin.

The boomerang should fly out-ward about 25 yards, circle to the left, move from the vertical to the horizontal and return to you in a gentle hover. Once you've accomplished some accurate returns, you're ready to attempt a catch. As it planes down to you at chest height, grasp the boomerang between your palms, one above the other.

The symmetry of the boomer-ang's flight is now complete—the thrower has become the catcher.

MICHAEL LAMM

**FICTION:** You need to have a strong arm to throw a boomerang.

**FACT:** Finesse counts much more than power.

HOLLY ENGLISH PAYNE

# ANATOMY

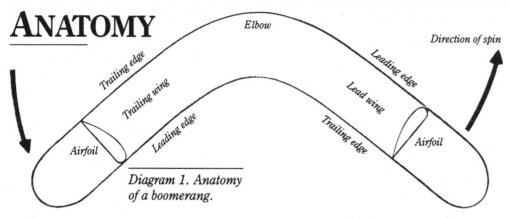

Diagram 1. Anatomy of a boomerang.

Before we go into more detail on throwing and catching, let's analyze the anatomy of the boomerang.

The classic boomerang consists of a lead wing and a trailing wing joined at the elbow. Each wing has a leading edge and a trailing edge, oriented so the leading edges strike the air in turn as the boomerang rotates in flight. The wings are usually equal in length and straight or slightly tapered toward the tips, so that in cross-section they resemble the airfoils of airplane wings. The angle between the wings is typically 105° to 110°.

The origins of this configuration predate history, but the functional reasons are still quite clear. Most boomerangs were made from the junction of a tree and its lateral root. The angle of this junction tends to be slightly more than 90°, hence the angle of the boomerang. The tapered tips are a carryover from the boomerang's parent, the killer-stick. Neither the angle nor the tapered tips are ideal for a sporting

boomerang, although they were perfect for a killer-stick—offering high tip speed and concentrated impact on contact with game.

Modern materials have allowed many configurations of boomerangs to be explored, and very successful models have been made with angles between wings varying from less than 45° to more than 120°.

The polypropylene Darnell boomerang, designed by co-author Eric Darnell.

The lightweight, polypropylene Darnell boomerang incorporates many refinements above and beyond the classic shape:

∧ The wingtips are bulbous and rounded to provide a good grip on the launch and to ensure safer catches.

The flared tips also stabilize the boomerang's flight by adding more weight to its extremities.

∧ The wings are unequal in length, which helps slow the spin at the end of the flight for easier catching.

∧ The angle between the wings, roughly 75°, moves the center of rotation away from the elbow and effectively lowers the tip speed.

∧ The lead wing has a pronounced undercut, allowing this boomerang to fly like a wooden one.

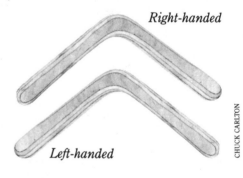

Right-handed

Left-handed

*All boomerangs are either right- or left-handed.* One is the mirror opposite of the other; that is, the airfoils on the wings are reversed, as shown in the photograph above.

A right-hander launches a right-handed boomerang at a 50° angle to the right of the wind, so that it circles around back to the thrower in a counterclockwise direction. A southpaw launches a left-handed boomerang at the same angle to the left of the wind, so that it circles around in a clockwise ellipse.

# THE FLIGHT OF THE BOOMERANG

We can describe the classical boomerang as consisting of two wings joined at an angle, with airfoils that rotate in the same direction—rather like two helicopter rotor blades rotating after each other through the air. When launched vertically with sufficient spin and forward momentum, the boomerang reacts to gyroscopic forces that cause it to circle around and lay down as it returns, until it descends in a horizontal hover.

Few mechanical devices demonstrate so many laws working together. During the course of its flight, singly or in concert, the following principles come into play: Bernoulli's law, Newton's laws of motion, gyroscopic stability, gyroscopic precession (the "nohands" bicycle turn phenomenon), and several other laws of aerodynamics.

To unravel the principles governing its flight, let us first analyze how the elements of the boomerang work together to make it return.

*A boomerang's wings generate lift.* Bernoulli's principle states that air traveling at higher speed creates less pressure than air traveling at lower speed. The airfoil shape of a boomerang's wing applies this principle to create lift. The air passing over the curved top of the wing in diagram 2 has to go faster than the air going under the flat bottom to arrive at the back of the wing at the same time. This creates less pressure on the top of the wing than on the bottom, causing the wing to want to rise up toward the direction of less pressure. This is called "lift."

---

*Diagram 2. Bernoulli's principle at work.*

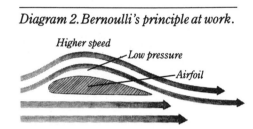

*Higher speed*  
*Low pressure*  
*Airfoil*

You can experiment with lift by putting your hand out the window of a moving car. While not a true airfoil, your hand will feel the force of the wind acting on it and a very small change in the angle of your hand will result in a large change in the direction it will want to move. The faster the car goes, the more pronounced the effect.

*The mass (weight) of a boomerang sustains its flight.* According to Newton's law of inertia, a body in motion tends to stay in motion; another Newtonian principle states that the resultant action of a force is directly proportional to the applied force minus friction and other resistant losses.

Thus a boomerang must have sufficient mass to absorb the inertia of your throw and to translate it into the momentum needed to carry out its flight. It will, however, be forced back to earth in a relatively short time because of the forces of drag on its airfoils (friction), wind resistance and gravity.

*The configuration of a boomerang's wings generates a stable spinning motion.* The length of the wings and the angle at which they are joined enable a boomerang to spin in a stable plane as a result of the spin imparted on the launch. This is called "gyroscopic stability." A gyroscope is nothing more than an object that spins on its axis, and gyroscopic stability is the tendency of a spinning object to continue spinning on its axis while *resisting* any force that attempts to change that axis.

*The combination of lift and spin causes the turn.* So the boomerang is stable, spinning rapidly, and is moving forward from the force of your launch. The turning force originates in the unequal airspeeds of the boomerang's spinning wings.

Back to Bernoulli: each wing (wing A in diagram 3, page 24), as it rotates forward into the direction of flight, creates more lift (because of the higher wind speed passing over it) than the wing rotating backward away from the direction of flight (wing B in diagram 3). The maximum force of lift is created near the 12 o'clock position.

Let's suppose for a moment that the boomerang isn't rotating at all, but is locked in the position shown in diagram 3. If it's whizzing through the air *but not spinning,* then clearly wing A is generating much more lift because it's facing the direction of flight whereas wing B is facing away from the direction of flight and generating less lift. In such a case, wing A would simply flip the boomerang over in the direction in which the force of lift is pushing. *(Cont.)*

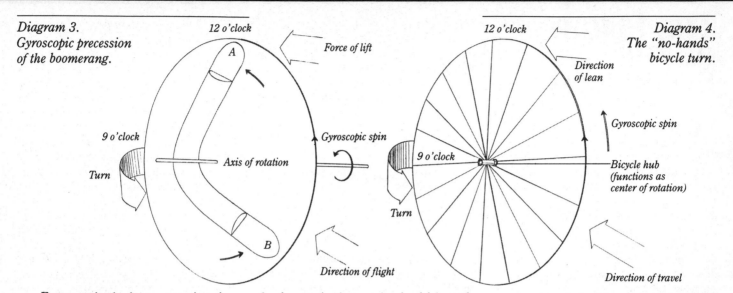

Diagram 3.
Gyroscopic precession
of the boomerang.

12 o'clock

A

Force of lift

9 o'clock

Gyroscopic spin

Axis of rotation

Turn

B

12 o'clock

Diagram 4.
The "no-hands"
bicycle turn.

Direction
of lean

Gyroscopic spin

9 o'clock

Bicycle hub
(functions as
center of rotation)

Turn

Direction of flight

Direction of travel

Fortunately the boomerang is spinning in gyroscopic bliss, so the result of the force of lift pushing at the 12 o'clock position on the gyroscopically stable, spinning boomerang is a reaction 90° later (at the 9 o'clock position). This reaction is a turn or change in the direction of flight.

This phenomenon is called "gyroscopic precession." A "no hands" turn on a bicycle works on the same principle (diagram 4). When you ride a bike, your forward motion makes the wheels rotate to create the gyroscopic spin that gives it stability at speed. When you lean into a "no hands" turn, the front wheel has a delayed reaction to the force of your lean: like all good gyroscopes, it turns 90° later than the point of applied force and 90° to the wheel. The result is a turn instead of a fall.

The bicycle turn and the boomerang turn differ from each other in that the former is the result of a fairly sudden strong force (your lean) producing a fairly abrupt turn, whereas the boomerang's turn is the result of a small force (lift) applied continually over the duration of the flight producing one large smooth turn (the boomerang's flight path). This turn is further complicated by the fact that the boomerang "lays down" in its flight as it returns to its source. You launch the boomerang with a nearly vertical tilt, yet it returns spinning horizontally like a record on a turntable.

There are two elements involved in the lay-down, both affecting the gyroscopic precession. The first element is that you launch the boomerang with a tilt and the precession maintains the tilt all the way around. You can imagine the boomerang traveling around on the inclined plane of a saucer (near the rim). This image would hold true if the boomerang traveled at a constant speed throughout its flight. But it doesn't, so enter the second element: momentum. When the boomerang leaves your hand, it has the maximum force applied to it and over the course of the flight it loses its momentum. Forward velocity and gyroscopic spin, the two forces at launch, are too great for precession to overcome them. As a matter of fact, if you look closely at a boomerang launched *hard*, you can see it go straight for a second before it starts its turn. As the boomerang continues its flight, it loses enough forward velocity for precession to start taking effect and the turn begins. Further in the flight, precession has become the dominant force, and the boomerang has not only turned but has progressively tilted over until it has laid down into a horizontal hover and descends to your waiting hands.

For this night shot photographer George Leavens outfitted a boomerang with three lamps, one at the center of gravity and one at each end, to illustrate its flight path. Launched vertically, the 'rang gradually "lays down" (see left of picture) on its return.

# FELIX HESS

## *A Space Age Scientist Zeroes In on the Stone Age*

In November 1968 *Scientific American* published an article that presented the boomerang as a Stone Age object worthy of Space Age attention—and ended up sparking the interest of aerospace wizards, physicists, engineers, pilots, hang-gliding enthusiasts, amateur ethnologists and people interested in anything Australian. The author of that article was a young Dutchman named Felix Hess, whose curiosity about boomerangs had begun during his undergraduate work in physics at the University of Groningen in Holland.

"I got interested when I learned that the behavior of boomerangs was not satisfactorily explained," Hess says. He went on to win a Ph.D. in 1973 after publishing a massive 555-page treatise titled *Boomerangs: Aerodynamics and Motion.* Written in English and filled with computer printouts of projected flight paths, the book comes complete with a viewing device to study certain double-image illustrations. It remains the definitive work on the subject and will probably never be rivaled. Copies are unavailable at stores since Hess's printer has vanished, along with the plates. Occasionally a student gets his

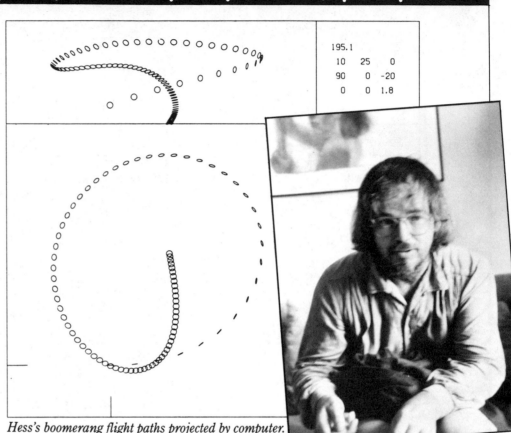

195.1

| 10 | 25 | 0 |
| 90 | 0 | -20 |
| 0 | 0 | 1.8 |

*Hess's boomerang flight paths projected by computer.*

BENJAMIN RUHE

hands on one of the few volumes extant and makes a copy for personal use, but this is daunting work.

Queried on what would happen if a boomerang were launched from an aerial balloon high in the sky, Hess used his computer to project a modest launch from 90 meters. In the simulated flight, the boomerang makes its turn, describes a small circle and drops down to the launch point. Then, because there is no ground to hit, it falls

and falls and gradually opens up a circle until it achieves approximately its original orbit. Taking energy from gravity, it spins and spins in a free fall that resembles the autumnal plunge of a maple seedpod.

When last heard from, Hess had finally exhausted the boomerang as a subject for scientific research and was happily embarked on a brand-new project: studying the mating calls of the Papua–New Guinea frog.

# CHECKING YOUR BOOMERANG

A boomerang is much more sophisticated than a Frisbee. It will not fly correctly if there's a twist or bend in one or both of its wings (unless you've programmed it for a special flight pattern, but that comes later), so checking your boomerang for straightness is a very important step before you go out to throw.

With the boomerang flat on a table, curved side up and wings facing away from you, press down on the elbow and observe the tips. When viewed from the end, the tips should be raised slightly ($\frac{1}{8}''$ to $\frac{1}{4}''$) off the surface and parallel to it. They should not be twisted except for built-in undercut (see diagram 5).

To verify this fairly flat, "neutral" position, tap the *tips* as you press down on the elbow. If the boomerang is in tune, the tips will move slightly and make a clacking sound. If a tip doesn't move, it may be bent down too far. Still pressing on the elbow, tap in the *middle* of the wing; if this produces movement, the wingtip needs bending up to the neutral position. If a wingtip is bent up too much ($\frac{1}{2}''$ or more), bend it down to the neutral position.

HOLLY ENGLISH PAYNE

*A wooden boomerang is heated over a steaming kettle in preparation for tuning.*

One of the many advantages of the polypropylene Darnell boomerang is that it can be tuned so easily. All you need to do is flex the wing beyond the desired warp and let it come back to the "set" position. The best way to tune a wooden boomerang is to apply some heat before warping. Hold the boomerang over a steaming kettle or electric or gas burner for 5 to 8 seconds, moving it constantly to keep the paint from blistering. Then remove it from the heat and apply the desired pressure until the boomerang sets. Wooden models can also be tuned by breathing heavily on the area to be bent and then holding the position for about 30 seconds until it sets; be very careful when using this method, as wooden boomerangs can break in the process.

*Diagram 5. Press down on the elbow to check your boomerang.*

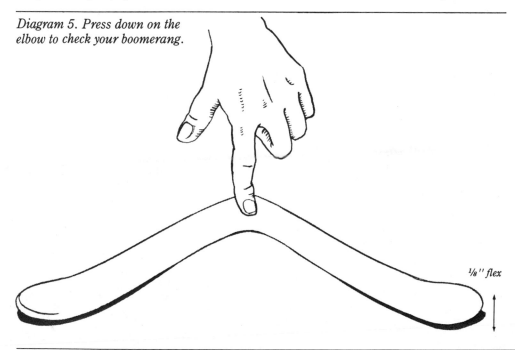

$\frac{1}{8}''$ flex

# WHERE TO THROW

Find a large, flat field, free of holes and obstructions (including trees and rocks). Keep your distance from houses, roads, automobiles and especially other people. The thrower should have a hundred yards of clear space in *all* directions, which means that crowded parks and beaches are off-limits for boomeranging. Before each throw, always check to see whether anyone has wandered into the vicinity of your throwing area.

# WHEN TO THROW

Wait for a calm day or evening to try out your boomerang. Early morning or just before sunset is generally a good time, because the wind tends to die down then. You will rarely have dead-calm conditions, but actually a little breeze gives the boomerang something to work against and makes throwing easier. A wind up to 12 mph is manageable; much above that, however, will cause problems with control. (If the wind is above 12 mph, go fly a kite!) Remember, the lighter the boomerang, the more wind affects it.

*Boomerangers need wide open spaces.*

# POSITION

Determine the direction of the wind by dropping a few blades of grass and observing which way they fall. Note that the wind at arm level may be lighter, and may be coming from a different direction, than wind above the tree tops. Waving branches and flapping flags can be misleading.

Imagine that the wind is coming from 12 o'clock. If you're a right-hander, face 2 o'clock to launch your boomerang. If you feel the wind on your left cheek, you're in the correct position. Almost all beginners tend to throw too much into the wind. Your boomerang will return to your left and behind you if this is the case. Left-handers (throwing left-handed boomerangs) do the mirror opposite of right-handers; that is, face 10 o'clock to launch.

MICHAEL MERCANTI, *PHILADELPHIA DAILY NEWS*

*American right-hander Barnaby Ruhe and Aussie left-hander Peter Maxwell illustrate correct launch positions in relation to the wind.*

*Diagram 6. Bird's-eye view of launch positions in relation to wind.*

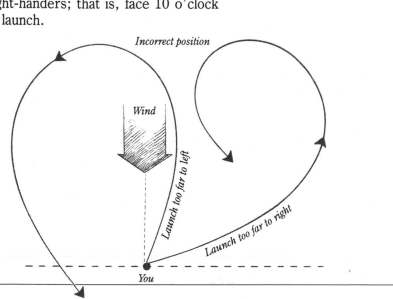

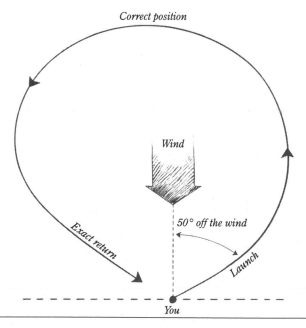

# GRIP

Pick up the boomerang so that the flat side is facing your palm. You can hold it by *either* wingtip as long as you use the appropriate grip. Most people hold the lead wing, which positions the "V" of the boomerang over the shoulder; this grip is used especially with the classic Aboriginal shape. The alternative, the "trailing wing grip" with the lead wing pointing behind the shoulder, sometimes gives beginners more control; this one is particularly appropriate for the Darnell boomerang. Try both to see which works best for you.

There are two basic ways to grasp the boomerang: the full grip and the pinch grip. For the full grip, hold the boomerang in the top of your hand, resting it on your little finger with your other fingers curled around it. The pinch grip can be used with any boomerang but is particularly appropriate for the smaller models. Try both.

Once you're outdoors, a sweaty palm, dew on the grass, drizzle—all may cause your boomerang to become slippery and hard to grasp. You can rub some dirt or a little rosin on your palms to alleviate the problem, but a more effective solution is to rub down the boomerang with a chamois cloth; this will give it a faintly tacky quality, which is ideal for achieving maximum spin on the launch. At the other end of the spectrum, you may be inconvenienced by overly dry hands on some days. Dust them with talcum powder or, alternatively, use some moisturizer. With rosin, chamois, powder and moisturizer in your bag, you have the beginnings of a professional boomeranger's kit.

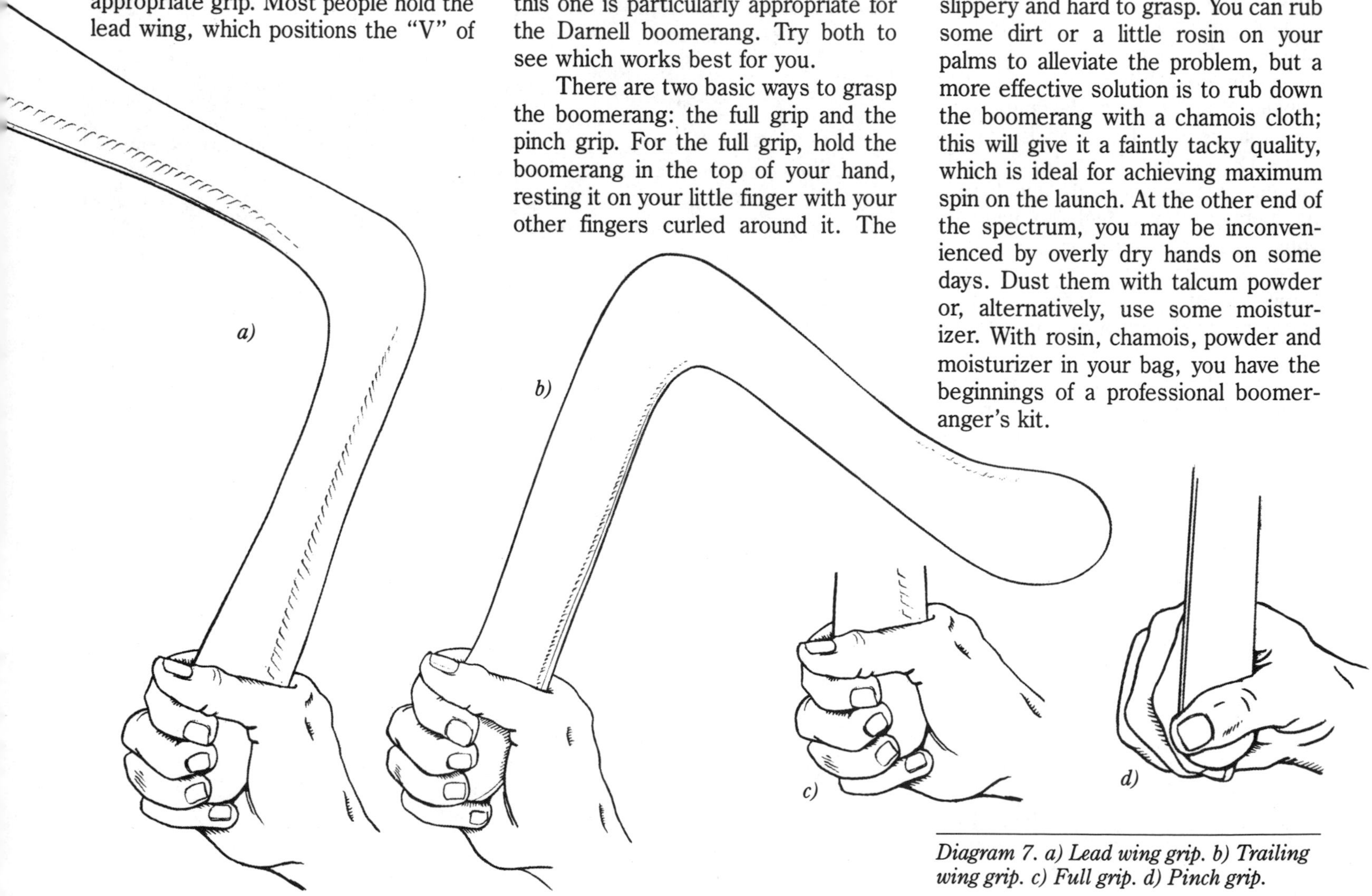

*Diagram 7. a) Lead wing grip. b) Trailing wing grip. c) Full grip. d) Pinch grip.*

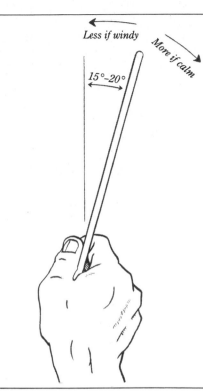

*Less if windy*

*More if calm*

15°–20°

*Diagram 8. Vertical tilt.*

# TILT

Hold the boomerang in a vertical position or nearly so, but never horizontally. This is the single most important rule to remember. One way to compensate for a tendency to throw sidearm is to tilt the boomerang slightly toward your head.

# AIM

Aim about 5° above eye level (15° above the horizon) or a little lower if the weather is very calm. If you have trouble visualizing this angle, try aiming at distant tree or house tops at least a hundred yards away and this

*Diagram 9. Point of aim at moment of release.*

**FICTION:** You throw a boomerang sidearm like a Frisbee, or you twist your wrist in the direction the boomerang will turn in flight to help it "round the circle."

**FACT:** Either of the above launches will end in disaster: the boomerang will soar up, stall, and come crashing down. Do this once too often and you'll have a two-piece 'rang.

The way to launch is with a nearly vertical tilt and straight out. Let "gyroscopic precession" take care of the turn and return.

should give you the correct angle of elevation. Be sure to release the boomerang at the point of aim, not above or below this level.

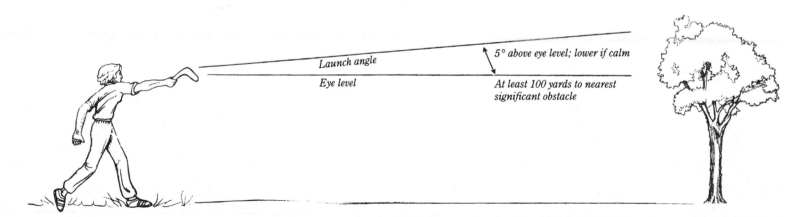

*Launch angle*

*5° above eye level; lower if calm*

*Eye level*

*At least 100 yards to nearest significant obstacle*

HOLLY ENGLISH PAYNE

# LAUNCH

With the boomerang cocked over your shoulder, step forward on the foot opposite to your throwing arm and simultaneously launch outward. Start with your arm bent at the elbow and end up with it extended as if you were snap-throwing a ball or cracking a whip. Remember to keep your upper arm close to your head during the entire action. Snap your wrist at the last moment, but don't open up your hand to let go of the boomerang. Rather, keep a firm grip on it as you throw outward. This will impart the all-important spin as it pulls out of your hand. The more spin, the better the throw and the more likely the boomerang will whir out as a gyroscope, climb a bit, lie down horizontally and circle around back to you in its unique flight pattern. Spin counts more than power, but remember to throw like you mean it and follow through with your arm and

*Diagram 10. Launch sequence.*

*Sight direction of launch; roll weight onto right foot*

*Step forward with left foot, wrist cocked back*

body. If you have difficulty adding enough spin to your throw, grip the boomerang snugly as you start the launch. Then, at the *instant* of release, grab the boomerang as tightly as you can. Don't worry about it sticking to your hand—it will pull itself free with loads of extra snap.

*Extend throwing arm overhead*

*Release, snap wrist and follow through*

## LEFT-HANDERS THROWING RIGHT-HANDED BOOMERANGS

L eft-handers can also throw right-handed boomerangs, like the one that comes with this book, by altering their grip and launch. Just grasp the boomerang with the *round* side facing the palm of your left hand, position yourself at a 50° angle to the *right* of the wind, and release the boomerang as though you're executing an overhand tennis smash. Lean your body a bit to the right to help you launch the boomerang with a slight tilt to the right. This maneuver basically simulates a right-handed throw.

*How to throw a right-handed boomerang, left-handed.*

33

# JOHN MCMAHON

## *"Billy Boomerang"*

To the tens of thousands of tourists who saw him in action over the years on the resort island of South Padre in southern Texas, and to the millions who viewed him in a tender CBS documentary by Charles Kuralt in his *On the Road* series, John McMahon indelibly linked boomerangs with freedom. A New Yorker who came to the island with the Coast Guard and stayed on, "Billy Boomerang," as he was widely known, needed a way to support his beachcombing lifestyle. As Kuralt puts it, the solution came to him "from out of the blue": boomerangs.

A former weightlifter, McMahon made the tossing look deceptively easy. With lots of spare time to practice and unlimited throwing space, he perfected his act until finally he could throw five boomerangs in a row and catch all five on return. Another trick involved holding three boomerangs in his right hand and one in his left, launching the four simultaneously and catching all of them on return. Consecutive catch was a personal fascination. He established his own record of 157 straight catches, which he later upped to 388—more than an hour's worth of continuous throwing.

McMahon crafted his boomerangs out of plywood, decorating many with religious motifs, and set up shop simply by sticking the tips into the sand near a jetty where boats delivered fresh batches of tourists. After giving a demonstration, McMahon dispensed free lessons and peddled his wares, which included shark's-tooth jewelry, a sideline from his scuba diving and fishing hobbies.

Until his death at age 47, McMahon made his living in this way. He was so widely known that his obituary was carried by UPI.

# TROUBLESHOOTING

## IF YOUR BOOMERANG...

| | |
|---|---|
| ∧ Lands to your left when you face the wind... | *Launch more to your right and a little lower.* |
| ∧ Lands to your right when you face the wind... | *Launch more to your left and a little higher.* |
| ∧ Hits the ground halfway around... | *Throw harder, with more snap. Also, tilt the boomerang a little bit from the vertical to the horizontal.* |
| If the boomerang still fails to return all the way back to you... | *Bend the tip of the lead wing up slightly but leave the trailing wing neutral. Keep bending and testing until it comes around properly.* |
| ∧ Skies upward and then pendulums downward at the end of the flight (instead of hovering down)... | *Launch the boomerang with more vertical tilt, throw outward slightly above eye level and follow through with your entire body.* |
| If the boomerang still climbs, then pendulums... | *Bend the tip of the lead wing down a little until a lower flight height is maintained.* |
| ∧ Dips downward and then zooms sharply upward... | *Launch higher, aiming at the distant treetops, and follow through with your throw.* |
| ∧ Flies upward, stalls a bit and swoops downward in a hump-backed trajectory... | *Launch lower and follow through with your throw.* |
| ∧ Comes back but keeps on going past... | *Ease up on the launch effort but not on the spin (snap of the wrist).* |
| ∧ Skims the grass all the way around... | *Launch slightly higher.* |
| ∧ Is thrown perfectly but the wind blows it 50 yards downwind... | *Go fly a kite!* |

# BASIC SANDWICH CATCH

When you begin to get good returns, try catching the boomerang. Start off with a light boomerang to develop your technique. The key to catching is in position and timing. Learn the flight path of your boomerang so you can be there facing it to make the catch. Don't attempt a grab if the boomerang comes in fast or pendulums down at a sharp angle; keep it in view and step aside to avoid being hit. A boomerang that slowly hovers down to you is the easiest to catch, as well it should be—it's doing exactly what it was meant to do. Watch the boomerang closely and let it drop down until it reaches chest height or lower. Hold out your hands horizontally, palms facing each other about 18 inches apart and fingers stiff.

Now trap the boomerang by clapping your palms together as it planes in between them and draw your arms in toward you.

Many people make successful catches after only a short practice session. Others will take a little longer. Once you experience the thrill of catching your own throw, however, you'll be hooked forever.

*Diagram 11. Basic sandwich catch, in theory and practice.*

# COPING WITH THE WIND

Boomeranging will turn you into an aerologist as you study the wind currents and atmosphere. Just as objects in the path of a body of water affect the flow rate and turbulence of the water, so buildings, trees and the shape of the land affect the flow rate and turbulence of the sea of air through which the boomerang sails. Winds up to 12 mph are easy enough to deal with, particularly if they are constant rather than gusty and shifting. Much above 12 mph calls for experience in dealing with the wind factor.

## MODIFYING YOUR THROW

The basic moderate wind throw requires launching more off the wind, with more vertical tilt, less power and more spin than a throw in calm conditions. This will keep the boomerang vertical longer so the wind can't get under it and make it "kite" up and away. Also, by throwing more softly, the power of the throw is used up going upwind, and the boomerang is literally being blown back to the thrower.

A second type of wind throw works well even in winds up to 30 mph. (Needless to say, only the expert should attempt to gain this mastery.) This is the humpback or triangular

*MICHAEL MERCANTI, PHILADELPHIA DAILY NEWS*

*Diagram 12. Triangular humpback throw.*

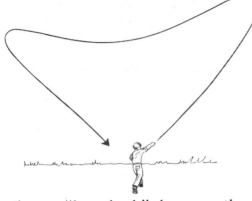

throw—"humpback" because the flight path has two high points instead of one, and "triangular" because it has two distinct turn points instead of a circular orbit. This throw requires that you launch almost 90° off the wind, with a fairly vertical tilt, aiming very high (almost 45° above the horizon), with lots of power and spin. The boomerang soars up to a peak that seems too far off the wind, then turns and dives across the wind, appearing destined for a crash, then rises to a second lower peak, turns and heads for home—arriving docilely enough for an easy grab. The harder you throw, the more vertical tilt you need. In the extreme case you may have to throw oververtically, i.e., with the 'rang tilted toward you.

# MODIFYING YOUR BOOMERANG

*Using a clunker.* You may choose to fly a small, heavy "clunker" boomerang— one that would barely fly in a light breeze. Every boomerang kit ends up with one of these.

*Tuning.* You can tune your 'rang for less lift by bending the lead wing down. This will help the boomerang fly lower—out of the wind, so to speak.

*Weighting.* You can weight up a trusty old boomerang by taping coins (dimes, nickels, quarters) to the underside of one or both wings to make the boomerang fly nearer to the ground. Try a variety of combinations, and experiment with their placement to test the effect. The closer the weights to the tips, the farther the boomerang will fly; the closer to the elbow, the more it will spin.

*Attaching wind foilers.* The trouble with throwing clunkers or weighted 'rangs is that they have considerable mass and tend to return at a pretty fast clip, making them no fun to catch. A more sane approach is to make spoilers or "wind foilers," so called because they are fashioned from aluminum-foil tape bent to form an adjustable flap. The wind foiler, about 2″ long and standing up about ¼″ in the fully extended position, is usually mounted on top of the lead wing about two-thirds of the way out toward the tip. If the wind dies down, simply bend the flap down a bit.

*Using a "night-rang"* (see page 65). The same boomerangs that have slots carved out to receive glowing Cyalume capsules are superb for wind throws. For normal daytime throwing, put tape over the slots (with or without the capsules in place) and your 'rang will behave in the usual way. When the wind comes up, remove the tape and capsule from the lead wing for more control. If the wind increases, take the tape and capsule out of the trailing wing and *voilà!*—less lift and more drag, the perfect wind 'rang.

*Diagram 13. Wind foilers.*

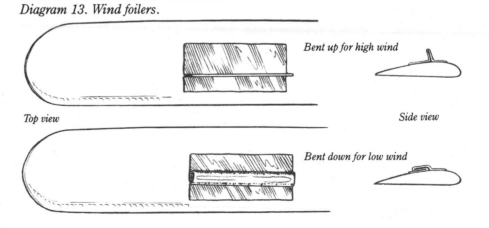

Bent up for high wind

Top view

Side view

Bent down for low wind

# Trick Throwing

## DOUBLING LAUNCH

Used in the Doubling competition, the simultaneous launch of two boomerangs from the same hand is the easiest of the trick throws. After all, if you can hurl one 'rang successfully, there's nothing to stop you from managing two at once. The only hazard here is the chance of midair collision of the two boomerangs. If this happens, try reversing them. Or grip them down at the tips and squeeze hard as you throw so that the wings will separate during the launch. You can also try putting a little bunch of grass between the two boomerangs right above the spot where you grip them; on the launch the 'rangs should separate sufficiently as the grass falls out of the way. If all else fails, try a different match of boomerangs.

*The Doubling throw: two boomerangs are launched from the same hand.*

GEORGE LEAVENS

HOLLY ENGLISH PAYNE

## ELBOW LAUNCH

This one is a bit harder. Use the pinch grip (see page 30) to grasp the boomerang by the elbow. Cock the boomerang back in your hand to yield as much spin as possible. Imparting a spin is essential with this launch, so be sure to snap your wrist vigorously.

*Diagram 14. Correct grip for the elbow launch.*

# RIGHT- AND LEFT-HANDED TOSSES

The demonstration thrower's domain begins with right- and left-handed tosses, executed one after the other as quickly as possible. A reasonable amount of ambidextrousness is required, so it makes sense to practice throwing with your off hand. Take a rightie and launch to the right of the wind, then pivot quickly to the left and throw the leftie left-handed to the left of the wind. The boomerangs will cross in flight for a pleasing pattern.

Now try a *simultaneous* right- and left-handed launch. Using lightweight, easy-to-throw, stable boomerangs, face *downwind* and throw the rightie to the left across your body and the leftie to the right across your body. Your wrists cross as though you're embracing someone. Test which suits you best: the right forearm crossing inside the left, or vice versa.

HOLLY ENGLISH PAYNE

*Eric Darnell demonstrates simultaneous throwing from the left and right hand.*

# BOOMERANGS ON THE LINE

In Waiyev, Fiji, at the 180° meridian that forms the International Dateline, it's possible to throw a boomerang *yesterday*, have it fly into the *today* zone and catch it *yesterday*. Or vice versa.

Chet Snouffer and friends of Delaware, Ohio, play their own tricks with time by launching their 'rangs just before the stroke of midnight on New Year's Eve, then catching them a few seconds later—in the following year.

Sailplane pilot Jim Johnson crossed four state lines with one throw when he stood at their juncture and winged his left-hander from New Mexico west over Arizona, north through Utah, east and south through Colorado, for the catch in New Mexico.

In Europe, on a visit to his wife's homeland, Australian Jackie Byham sailed a boomerang from Poland out over Russia and brought it back over the border under the suspicious eye of the Soviet guards.

The late Frank Donnellan, boomeranging legend of Sydney, Australia, laid his own life on the line when he launched a boomerang out the right-hand window of a moving car so that it came flying back through the opposite window for the traffic-stopping catch.

# TRICK CATCHING

## ONE-HANDED GRAB

Boomerangs, notably the omega designs (see page 57), create the illusion of circling around a "window" as they spin in flight. To catch one-handed, simply grab upward about shoulder height (elbow bent, palm facing up) and thrust your thumb through the "window" with outstretched fingers outside the circle. Make the move decisively, because at the slightest touch the boomerang will veer off sharply. Concentrate on keeping your eye on the boomerang. (Many people unknowingly either shut their eyes or turn away, thereby reducing their chances of success.) Of course, your goal is to make a clean grab, but hitting the boomerang without completing the catch will slow its spin and knock it up in the air a foot or two—giving you a second chance at a catch. Once you've mastered this with one hand, try the other.

If the boomerang comes in quite low, a downward grab may be needed. For this one, you must make a clean catch—there are no second chances.

Avoid making any catches—particularly one-handers—when the boomerang is coming in fast. Step aside and let it drop to the ground.

*The behind-the-back catch is often a partial body-trap.*

*"Just put out your hand and it will come to you."—Barnaby Ruhe*

## BEHIND-THE-BACK CATCH

Next in order of difficulty is the two-handed, behind-the-back catch. The goal here is to catch to the side, off the hip, so you can judge the flight of the boomerang as it comes in toward you. Wait till the boomerang has hovered down almost to eye level in front of you, then pivot around and catch it in both hands. Most behind-the-back grabs, because of the way the body is built, must be partial body-trap catches and are therefore permitted in competition.

## UNDER-THE-LEG CATCH

This one is quite a contortionist's trick. Extend your right arm well under your left leg, which is lifted high in the air, and make a standard two-handed (or one-handed) catch almost at knee level. Of course, left-handers do a mirror image of this.

JONATHAN SHERRILL

*Two members of the Ruhe/Ruhf clan show how it's done.*

MICHAEL LAMM

*Gymnast Chet Snouffer makes it look easy.*

## CATCH WITH THE FEET

The *pièce de résistance:* simulating the classic sandwich grab with your feet. Let the boomerang hover down low. When it's in its final hover, sit down within legs' reach of where the boomerang will land and clap it between your feet. Lean over on one side so that one leg is above the other.

## FREESTYLING

Trick catching has another, flashy dimension—what the Frisbee players call "freestyling." The object here is to perform twists and leaps in the air—even somersaults if you're able to do them—while negotiating the catch.

Your routine can be impromptu, with the catch matching the type of return the boomerang is making. One player, Red Whittington of Pittsburgh, can do two and a half twists in the air while snagging his boomerang on its return.

> **❝**Boomerangs are, without a doubt, the most utterly useless, intellectually satisfying objects ever devised by Stone Age minds for 20th-century appreciation. From the point of aerodynamics, kinetic poetry, or pure recreation, they are marvelous flying machines.**❞**
> —STEVE HALL

**66**May the fleas of a hundred wombats live forever in the armpits of any dingo who copies the boomerangs of another bloke.**99**

*—Lorin Hawes, discussing the problem of boomerang-design theft in his adopted Australian tongue*

# MAKING YOUR OWN

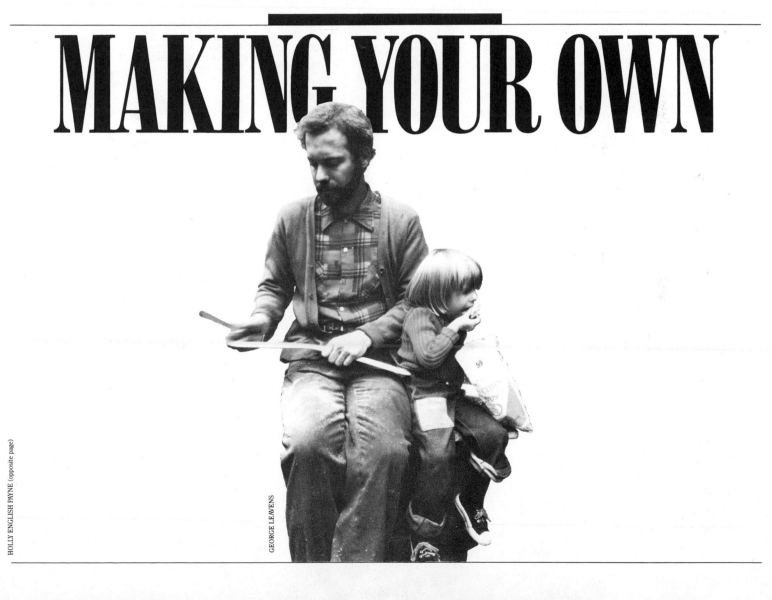

OW THAT YOU'RE WELL versed in throwing and catching the boomerang, it's time to consider making your own. Each of the six models shown in this chapter has been selected for its ease of construction as well as for its special flight properties. Complete all six and you'll have the beginnings of a well-stocked boomeranging kit.

The first two plans are for models that take no more than an hour or so to assemble: the cardboard three-blader is a fun indoor boomerang, guaranteed to liven up a rainy Saturday afternoon, while the wooden four-blader is great for backyard use. The remaining four plans—a classic Aboriginal shape, a wind-fighting omega, a mini-rang for high performance in a small space, and a maximum-time-aloft boomerang—call for slightly more sophisticated crafting but generously reward the effort that goes into their construction.

Since the cardboard three-blader, wooden four-blader and mini-rang can be used in smaller areas than those referred to in the Safety Rules (page 20), care and common sense are essential in adapting these rules to the circumstances.

**FICTION:** Wood is the only material for boomerangs.

CHUCK CARLTON

**FACT:** While wood was the only material available to the Australian Aborigines, modern-day boomerangs have been constructed successfully from pressed paper, cardboard, cloth laminates, bone, metal (aluminum and stainless steel), carbon fibers, bamboo, fiberglass, plexiglass (for the "seethrumarang"), nylon, styrofoam, a variety of other plastics such as polypropylene—and composites of the above.

The polypropylene Darnell boomerang that comes with this book has higher weather-resistance and more flexibility than its plywood counterparts, it lasts longer and is less likely to hurt when caught or to break when thrown incorrectly.

GEORGE LEAVENS

# TOOLS

Some or all of the
following tools will
be needed when you
make boomerangs from
the plans in this chapter.

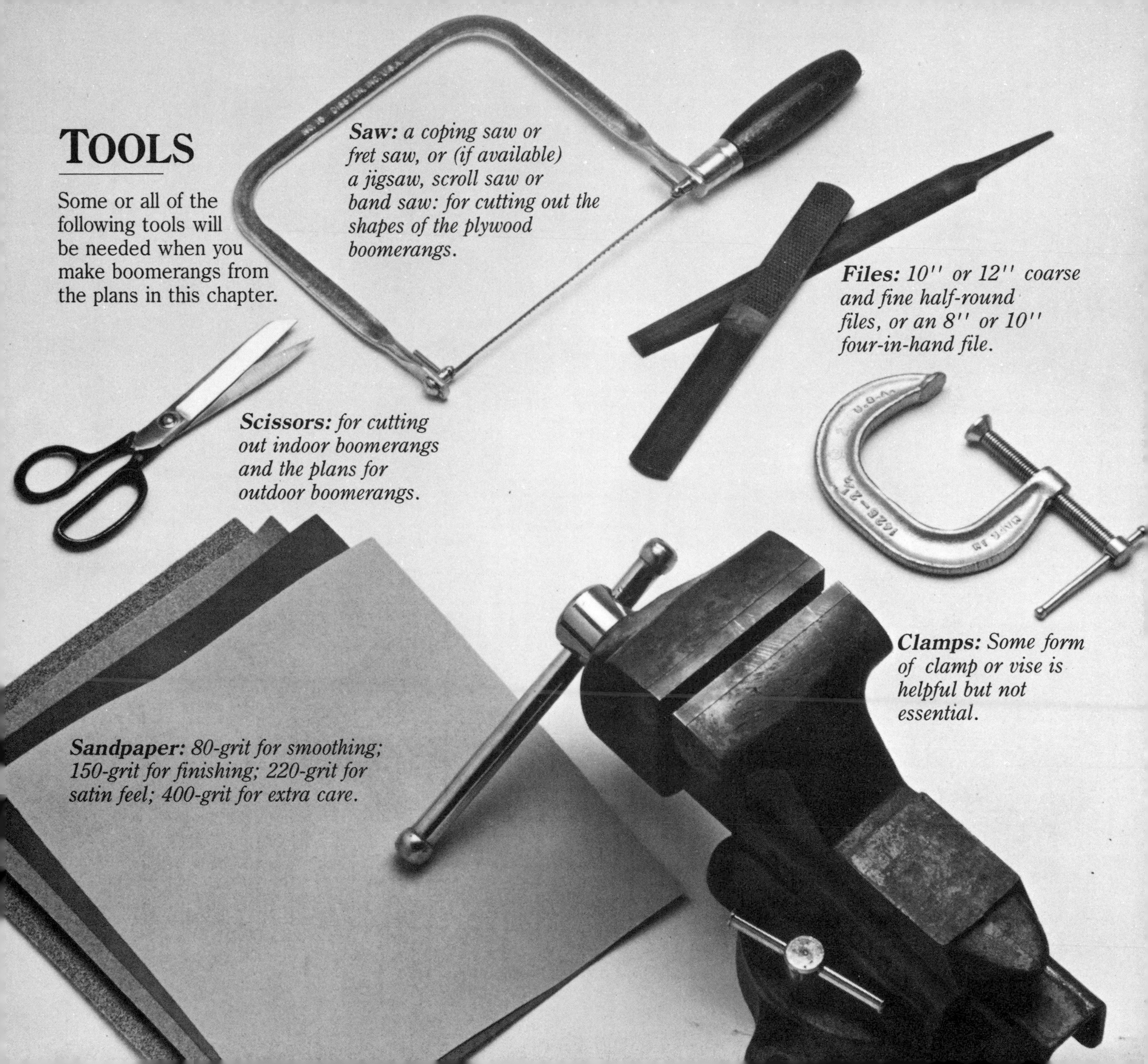

**Saw:** *a coping saw or
fret saw, or (if available)
a jigsaw, scroll saw or
band saw: for cutting out the
shapes of the plywood
boomerangs.*

**Files:** *10'' or 12'' coarse
and fine half-round
files, or an 8'' or 10''
four-in-hand file.*

**Scissors:** *for cutting
out indoor boomerangs
and the plans for
outdoor boomerangs.*

**Clamps:** *Some form
of clamp or vise is
helpful but not
essential.*

**Sandpaper:** *80-grit for smoothing;
150-grit for finishing; 220-grit for
satin feel; 400-grit for extra care.*

*Diagram 15. Cardboard three-blader.*

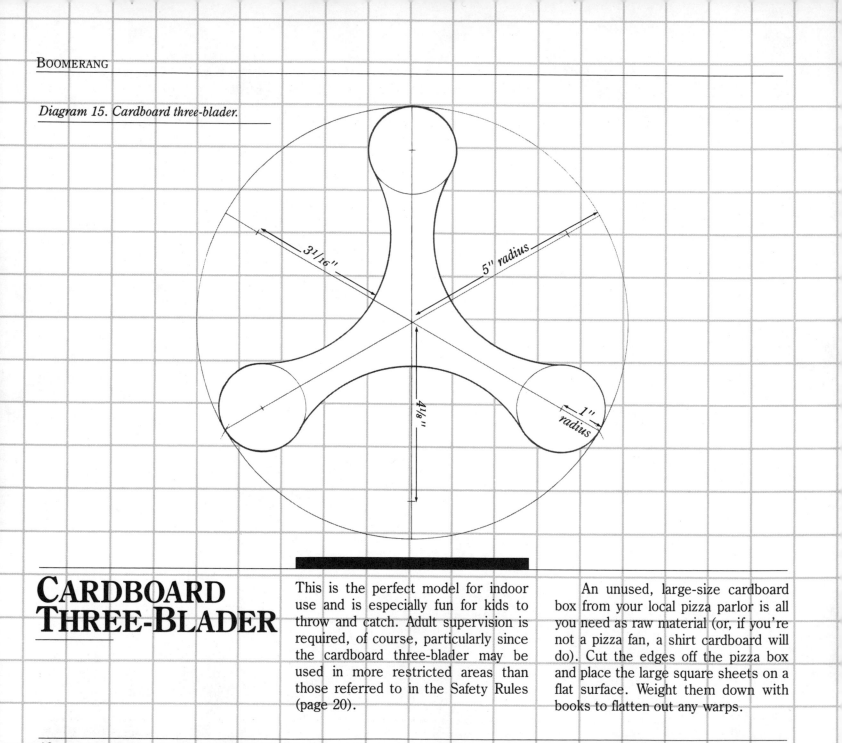

31/16"

5" radius

4 1/8"

1" radius

# CARDBOARD THREE-BLADER

This is the perfect model for indoor use and is especially fun for kids to throw and catch. Adult supervision is required, of course, particularly since the cardboard three-blader may be used in more restricted areas than those referred to in the Safety Rules (page 20).

An unused, large-size cardboard box from your local pizza parlor is all you need as raw material (or, if you're not a pizza fan, a shirt cardboard will do). Cut the edges off the pizza box and place the large square sheets on a flat surface. Weight them down with books to flatten out any warps.

# CONSTRUCTION

**1** Using a compass, draw a 10″ circle on a separate sheet of paper and mark the center (see diagram 15).

**2** Draw a line through the center, dividing the circle in half.

**3** With the compass still set on 5″, put the center at one end of the bisecting line and mark off two points on the circle (one on each side of the line). From each of these points draw a line through the center to the other side of the circle. You have now divided the circle into six equal parts.

**4** On every other line, mark 1″ from the edge of the circle. With your compass set on 1″, put the center at the 1″ mark and draw a 2″ circle on each of these three legs so that it just touches the line of the larger circle.

**5** On the remaining three lines, measure 4⅛″ out from the center and mark those points. Then, with the center at each of those three points, set your compass on 3¹/₁₆″ and swing an arc connecting the 2″ circles you drew on the other three legs.

**6** Cut out the shape defined by the darker lines on the plan and you have the pattern for an indoor three-bladed boomerang.

**7** Now back to the cardboard sheets. To find the grain (yes, even cardboard has grain), hold each sheet by opposite edges and flex it slightly. Then rotate it 90° and try again. When it flexes with the least resistance, the edges you're holding run parallel to the grain.

**8** Place your pattern on the cardboard so that one wing is lined up with the grain (see diagram 16). Trace around the pattern and cut out carefully. You should be able to get several boomerangs out of the top piece and several more out of the bottom piece of a large pizza box.

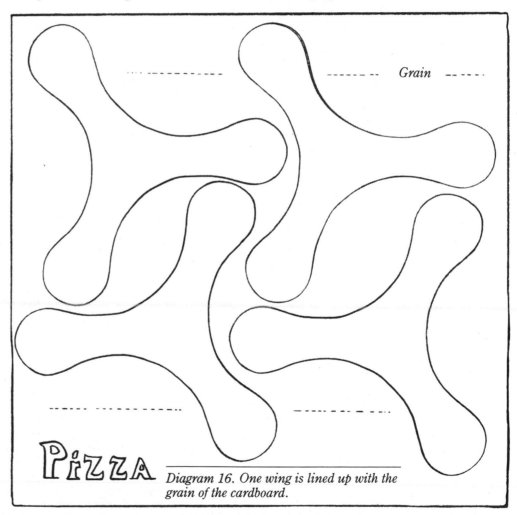

*Grain*

Pizza

*Diagram 16. One wing is lined up with the grain of the cardboard.*

## TUNING

Place the cut-out boomerang on a table and check to see whether the cardboard is warped. If it is, gently smooth the twists until the piece lies flat. Be careful not to kink the cardboard as you straighten it.

To tune the boomerang, gently bend the wings so the tips are about ⅛″ to ¼″ off the table with the center still flat. This flexed position, called the dihedral, gives the cardboard boomerang stability in its hover. Remember, the side with the tips flexed up is the top of the 'rang.

Now, if you want your boomerang to be a right-hander, take a wing that is pointing toward you and twist it up on the right-hand side. This will give a positive angle of attack. Move each of the other two wings to face you and twist them the same way. Very little twisting is necessary to achieve the desired effect. To make a left-hander, do just the opposite: with each wing pointed toward you, twist up the left-hand side.

## THE THROW

Hold the boomerang with a pinch grip (see diagram 7 on page 30). Your thumb should be in the middle of one wingtip as you press the boomerang against the side of your index finger opposite the last knuckle. This is an indoor boomerang, so there is no wind to work against and you should throw a little more sidearm (about a 45° tilt)

than you would outdoors. Cock the boomerang back in your hand, cock your wrist back, and cock your arm back. Then throw low, snapping your wrist for extra spin. The boomerang should zip out, spinning smartly, then swoop up to a high point and circle back into a hover in front of you.

## COMBO THREE-BLADER

Now for a treat. You can make a terrific short-range outdoor boomerang out of two of your indoor 'rangs and three dimes. First Scotch-tape a dime in the center of each tip of one 'rang, then lay a second 'rang on top to sandwich the dimes. Tape the two 'rangs together at the tips and at the waist of each wing (see diagram 17). Now tune your new combination boomerang the same way as for the single-thickness three-blader and head out for some fun. Subtlety in tuning is the key to success here. Throw to the right of the wind if you're right-handed (lefties opposite) and launch outward, keeping the boomerang very vertical. For more details on throwing and catching, see pages 28 to 36.

*Diagram 17. Cardboard combination boomerang. (Thickness not to scale.)*

Coin

Tape

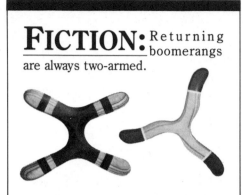

**FICTION:** Returning boomerangs are always two-armed.

**FACT:** Boomerangs can have two, three, four, five or six arms. They can be shaped to resemble most of the alphabet letters, as well as tomahawks, straight-edge razors, kangaroos and even the human figure. Assuming that correct aerodynamic principles are followed, all these designs can be constructed to fly well and return nicely.

CHUCK CARLTON

# HERB SMITH
## *The Man Who Reinvented the Boomerang*

When he first became interested in how boomerangs fly, premier British archer Herb Smith found that visits to the British Museum in London yielded little practical help—even though their collection bulged with Australian Aboriginal objects. Having in his mind's eye the rudimentary crescent shape of a boomerang from illustrations out of books, Smith set to making his own. He experimented and persevered, and eventually figured out the essentials: two airplane wings of correct proportions joined at the elbow at an acute angle, plus a vertical throw against the wind.

A short but exceedingly strong man, Smith was drawn to long-distance throwing. Experimenting with the strong prevailing winds of his home county, Sussex, he learned by trial and error that weighting his boomerang's wingtips, to increase inertia, would produce the range he desired. After repeatedly getting his boomerangs to fly out 100 yards or more and return accurately, Smith was ready. On June 17, 1972, he organized a platoon of Little-hampton Sports Club members as officials and pulled off a throw of 108 yards with complete and accurate return. This carefully documented event qualified him for *The Guinness Book of World Records*.

Acquiring an American sponsor, who had seen him on TV in England, Smith made it to the Smithsonian Institution's annual tournament in 1976 (the first of several visits) and wowed everyone with his winning personality and powerful throwing. His Gem, Sycamore, Traditional, Hook and weighted long-range models, all original designs, set performance and craftsmanship standards rarely equaled since. A prison warden by profession, Smith showed off a few boomerangs of his own design that had been elegantly hand-lettered with the words "Sussex Hook" by one of his convicts—a man described by one judge as "the second best forger in England."

Smith has written a book titled *Boomerangs: Making and Throwing Them,* which shares all his hard-won knowledge. "I am fully confident," he concludes, "that the reader of this modest little book not only will be in a position to make and throw his own boomerangs successfully, but will no doubt be able to improve on my own humble achievements."

HOLLY ENGLISH PAYNE

*Diagram 18. Wooden four-blader.*

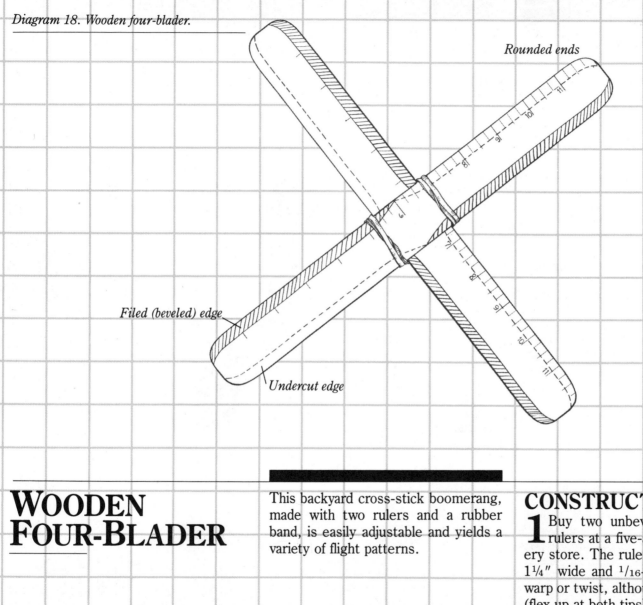

Rounded ends

Filed (beveled) edge

Undercut edge

# WOODEN
# FOUR-BLADER

This backyard cross-stick boomerang, made with two rulers and a rubber band, is easily adjustable and yields a variety of flight patterns.

## CONSTRUCTION

**1** Buy two unbeveled 12″ wooden rulers at a five-and-ten or stationery store. The rulers should be about 1¼″ wide and $1/16$–$1/8$″ thick with no warp or twist, although a little dihedral (flex up at both tips) is fine.

**2** Some rulers have a metal strip along one edge. This must be removed and the groove filled with glue.

**3** File the top left-hand side of each ruler as far as the 6″-mark, then switch ends and file the other left-hand side up to the 6″-mark. Now turn each ruler over, repeat the process on the other side and round all ends. These instructions and diagrams are for a right-handed boomerang; if you want a left-hander, file down the right-hand side of each ruler.

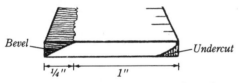

*Diagram 19. Enlarged cross-section of ruler, showing profile after shaping.*

Bevel — Undercut
¼″ — 1″

**4** Smooth the rulers with 220-grit sandpaper.

**5** Double up a medium-weight 3″-long rubber band and slip it over the end of one of the rulers about three inches along.

**6** Place the middle of the second ruler flat against the first ruler between the rubber band and the end (see diagram 20).

**7** Stretch the rubber band over the middle of the second ruler and around the end of the first.

**8** Slide the second ruler along to the middle of the first ruler and center both. You are now ready for the maiden flight.

*Diagram 20. The three assembly steps.*

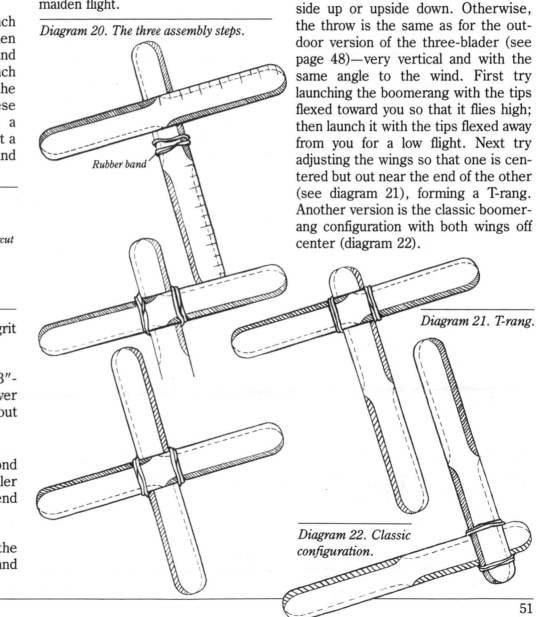

Rubber band

*Diagram 21. T-rang.*

*Diagram 22. Classic configuration.*

## THE THROW

The unique shaping of this cross-stick boomerang allows it to be thrown right side up or upside down. Otherwise, the throw is the same as for the outdoor version of the three-blader (see page 48)—very vertical and with the same angle to the wind. First try launching the boomerang with the tips flexed toward you so that it flies high; then launch it with the tips flexed away from you for a low flight. Next try adjusting the wings so that one is centered but out near the end of the other (see diagram 21), forming a T-rang. Another version is the classic boomerang configuration with both wings off center (diagram 22).

# PLYWOOD MODELS

CHUCK CARLTON

*The four plywood models that can be made from plans in this book (from top to bottom): MTA, classic two-blader, omega and mini-rang.*

Having whetted your appetite, let's spread a little aerodynamic lift onto some plywood. Before you start cutting out your boomerang shape, you first have to get the right grade of plywood and scale up the plans in the book.

## PLYWOOD SOURCES

By far the best material to use is premium-grade, cabinetmaker's plywood. You want 5-ply (which means 5 layers of wood are pressed together) with ¼″ (5 or 6mm) thickness, unless stated otherwise in the plan. This type is generally marketed as Finnish or Baltic birch plywood. You should be able to find the right quality at a cabinetry shop or good lumber supply house. Otherwise, you can get it via mail order. To obtain a list of suppliers, write the United States Boomerang Association, P.O. Box 2146, Lower Burrell, Pa. 15068. Enclose $1 and a large, stamped, self-addressed envelope to cover costs.

## SIZING

All the plywood boomerangs on the following pages have been drawn against a grid, with each box representing one square inch. Take this book to a photocopy center equipped with zoom enlarging and reducing machines, and ask for the drawings to be enlarged so that the box intervals are close to 1″. But why stop there? These "full-size" drawings are only guidelines. While you're at the store, have some in-between and giant sizes made up for future use. If you're feeling particularly ambitious, you can, of course, scale up these plans at home.

All the plans in this book are for right-handed boomerangs. If you want to make left-handed versions, just hold the blown-up copy against a window with light behind it and trace the lines through the paper. Mark the original side *right* and traced side *left,* and save them for your files.

## CONSTRUCTION

**1** Put a photocopy of the model you've chosen to build on a sheet of plywood with a piece of legal-size carbon paper (dark side down) inserted between the two. Instead of using carbon paper, you can also scribble on the back of your plan with a graphite pencil to transfer your image onto the plywood. All thin plywood comes warped, so be sure the *concave* side is facing up. This will give the correct flex to your boomerang's wingtips.

**2** Trace the outline onto the plywood and cut out the shape with your saw (see diagram 23).

**3** File this rough model to make the sloped edges specific to your chosen design. If you look at a cross-section of a boomerang, you'll see that it's flat underneath and rounded on top. This creates its basic airfoil shape. In addition to its own wing design, each model has a unique set of airfoils. As you file, the layers (or lamination lines) that make the airfoils will become apparent. The lines on each plan represent the desired configuration of these plywood layers in the finished boomerang. Note that the trailing edges have gentler slopes than the leading edges, with a transition occurring at the elbow. This means you take more off the trailing edges than the leading edges.

**4** With a finer file, smooth out any bumps in the edges and tips. The layers of thin-veneer plywood splinter easily, so take care to file only *toward* the edge (see diagram 24).

**5** Finally, round all the edges and finish up with 80-, 150- and 220-grit sandpaper.

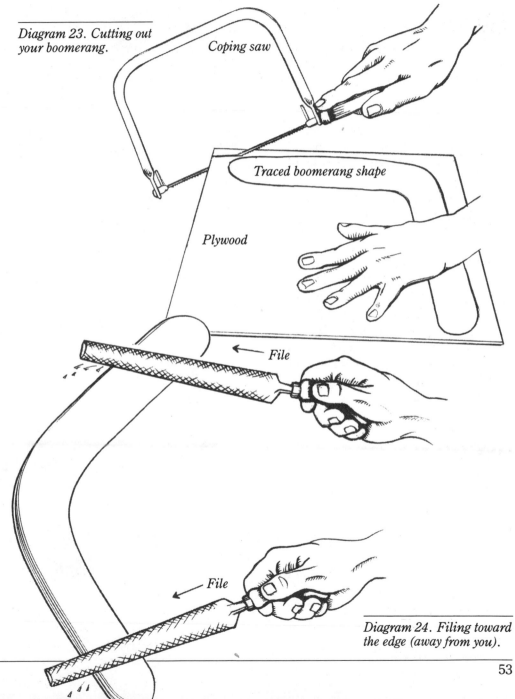

*Diagram 23. Cutting out your boomerang.*

Coping saw

Traced boomerang shape

Plywood

← File

← File

*Diagram 24. Filing toward the edge (away from you).*

## TESTING

Before you fly it, put the boomerang on the table and check for warp and dihedral (flexed tips). A little positive dihedral is good ($\frac{1}{8}''-\frac{1}{4}''$) at the tips when you push down on the elbow of the boomerang. Any twist on the wings, however, should be removed by following the directions in the section on checking (page 27).

Now head out for a couple of test tosses. Refer to the how-to-throw instructions (pages 28 to 36) to be sure you're doing everything correctly. If your boomerang doesn't return, even after careful tuning, it may be because you haven't carved it accurately. Check over the plans again and make sure you've filed all the edges as shown and sanded all the surfaces to a smooth finish. Rough edges can negatively affect the boomerang's flight pattern.

## DECORATING AND FINISHING

Once you've test-flown your boomerang, you're ready to add the final touches. For inspiration, feast your eyes on the boomerangs pictured on this page. There are four basic guidelines to keep in mind:

**1** Resand the boomerang after testing and before finishing.

**2** Use bright colors. They make the boomerang much easier to see in the air and on the ground.

**3** Use restraint when applying paint or varnish, as thick coats add unwanted weight. Apply two coats and sand well between each coat.

**4** After staining or painting, add a thin final coat of good exterior-grade urethane.

*Models (with designers) from Eric Darnell's and Ben Ruhe's collections: From top to bottom: Admiral's Hat (Les and Arthur Janetski); Super F-rang (Larry Ruhf); Hook (Peter Cashin); Inside Hat (Larry Ruhf).*

CHUCK CARLTON

# RUSTY HARDING
## *Boomerang Engineer*

**"S**omeone once said that analyzing a boomerang's flight is more difficult than analyzing a flight to the moon and back," says Rusty Harding, the leading boomerang theoretician in the United States. "And it's true. The variables affecting the flight of the boomerang are more complex."

This is no pie-eyed poet of the boomerang talking. Harding worked as a project engineer on the Boeing 747, among other airplanes, and designed control systems for the Minuteman missile before dropping out of the California aerospace industry "to gain control of my life again." His solution: adopt a simpler lifestyle, move where the living was cheaper, and start the small handicraft business that eventually centered on boomerangs.

Harding now lives in Carthage, Tennessee, where he sells all the boomerangs he can manufacture by hand. "I'd rather just continue making good boomerangs myself," he says, "maintaining the quality I feel is important and letting others mass-produce what they will. Besides, it's difficult to be a design leader, which I want to be, when your tail is tied to a few high-production-rate designs. I'll not stop experimenting or stop introducing new designs as I continue to learn."

Harding became acquainted with

GEORGE LEAVENS

boomerangs in the 1940s when a relative brought one back from Australia. Then he saw an advertisement in a magazine and, as a southpaw, bought three left-handed models. When his family wanted to throw, too, he turned out some right-handers for them and soon found himself making extras for the people who came to watch the Hardings at play.

Hearing that the Smithsonian Institution ran an annual tournament, he wrote for details ("Suddenly a whole new world of information opened up to me") and attended the next Smithsonian fling. Then he experimented, read and corresponded with other boomerangers, until finally a line of beautifully crafted and decorated Harding boomerangs, made of high-grade 7-ply aircraft birch, was selling like hot cakes. Demand far exceeded supply, and Harding was firmly launched in a new career.

The Harding production boomerangs range from the straightforward EZ Floater (a basic chevron shape) to the Hurricane Hook, from a Napoleon Hat Mini (the omega shape scaled way down) to a whimsical Tomahawk (complete with rawhide wrapping to secure the "blade"). His limited issues occur in the shape of alphabet letters, a Sikh knife, a straight-edge razor, multi-bladers, and a tri-winged airplane ("the Red Baron"). His Concept series boomerangs are made of polished hardwood wings overlapped at the elbow, epoxied and pegged like finely crafted furniture.

Harding's by now encyclopedic knowledge of the complexities of boomerang flight has led him to make frequent lengthy contributions to boomerang periodicals around the world. He has codified all his knowledge into a manuscript, *The Boomerang Bible,* aimed at the connoisseur. For the future, he pledges to put his knowledge of computers to use by producing software on aspects of boomeranging.

*Diagram 25. Classic two-blader. (¼" or 5–6mm plywood)*

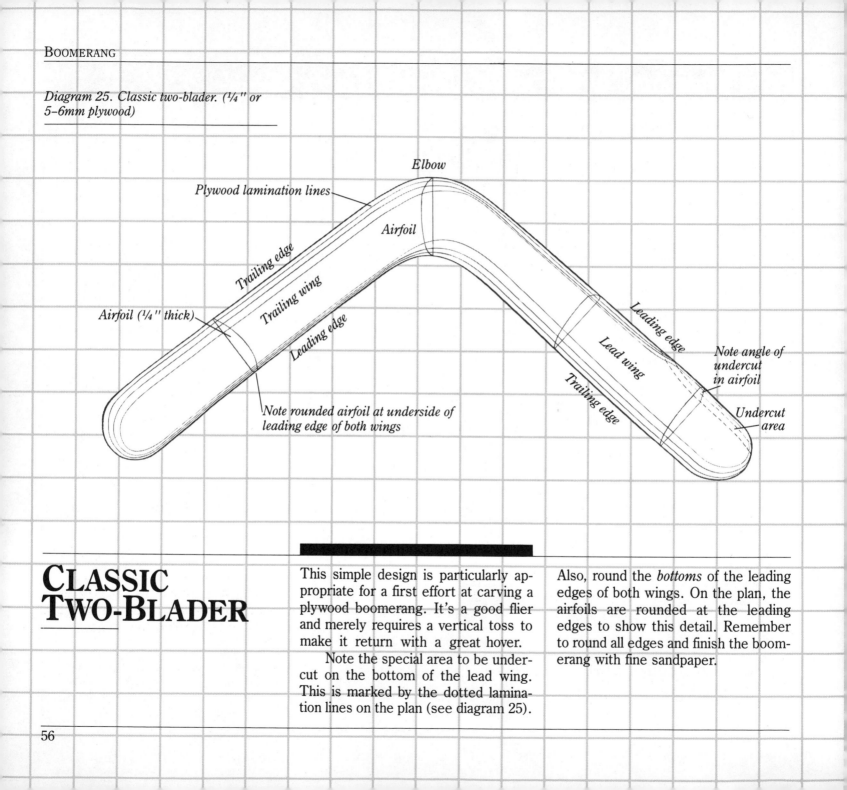

Plywood lamination lines

Elbow

Airfoil

Trailing edge

Trailing wing

Airfoil (¼" thick)

Leading edge

Leading edge

Lead wing

Note angle of undercut in airfoil

Trailing edge

Note rounded airfoil at underside of leading edge of both wings

Undercut area

# CLASSIC TWO-BLADER

This simple design is particularly appropriate for a first effort at carving a plywood boomerang. It's a good flier and merely requires a vertical toss to make it return with a great hover.

Note the special area to be undercut on the bottom of the lead wing. This is marked by the dotted lamination lines on the plan (see diagram 25).

Also, round the *bottoms* of the leading edges of both wings. On the plan, the airfoils are rounded at the leading edges to show this detail. Remember to round all edges and finish the boomerang with fine sandpaper.

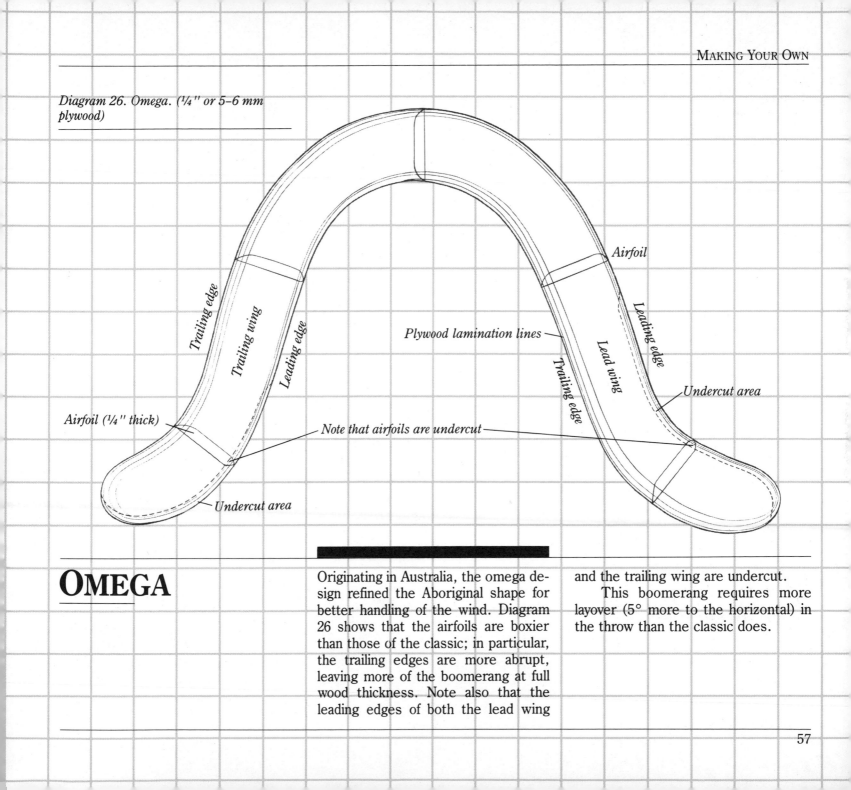

*Diagram 26. Omega. (¼" or 5–6 mm plywood)*

Airfoil

Leading edge

Lead wing

Trailing edge

Plywood lamination lines

Undercut area

Trailing edge

Trailing wing

Leading edge

Airfoil (¼" thick)

Note that airfoils are undercut

Undercut area

# OMEGA

Originating in Australia, the omega design refined the Aboriginal shape for better handling of the wind. Diagram 26 shows that the airfoils are boxier than those of the classic; in particular, the trailing edges are more abrupt, leaving more of the boomerang at full wood thickness. Note also that the leading edges of both the lead wing and the trailing wing are undercut.

This boomerang requires more layover (5° more to the horizontal) in the throw than the classic does.

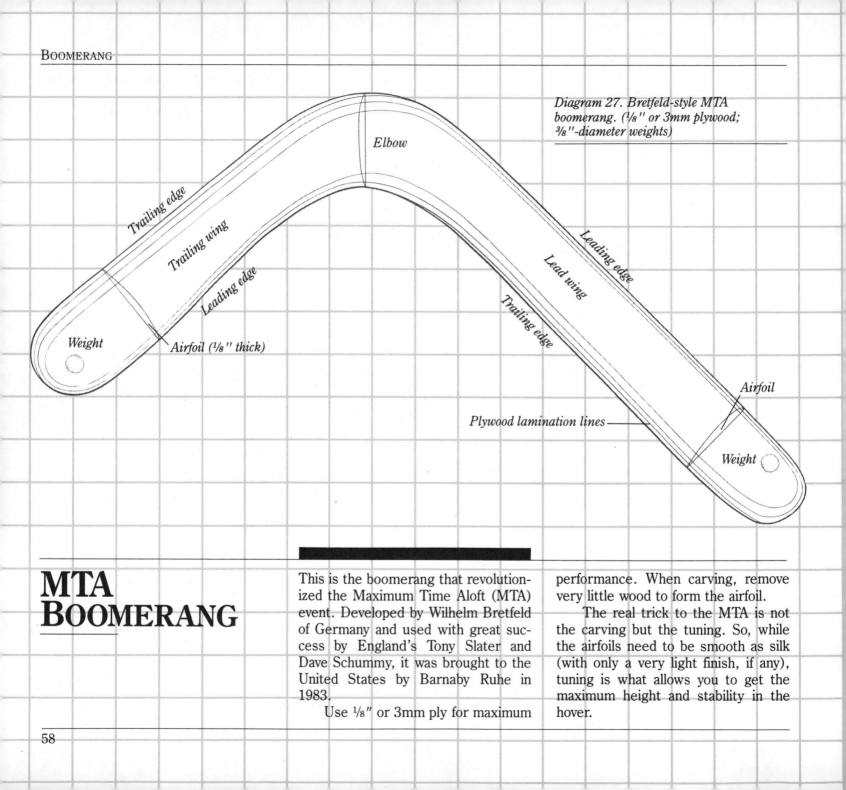

*Diagram 27. Bretfeld-style MTA boomerang. (⅛" or 3mm plywood; ⅜"-diameter weights)*

Trailing edge

Trailing wing

Leading edge

Elbow

Leading edge

Lead wing

Trailing edge

Weight

Airfoil (⅛" thick)

Airfoil

Plywood lamination lines

Weight

# MTA BOOMERANG

This is the boomerang that revolutionized the Maximum Time Aloft (MTA) event. Developed by Wilhelm Bretfeld of Germany and used with great success by England's Tony Slater and Dave Schummy, it was brought to the United States by Barnaby Ruhe in 1983.

Use ⅛" or 3mm ply for maximum performance. When carving, remove very little wood to form the airfoil.

The real trick to the MTA is not the carving but the tuning. So, while the airfoils need to be smooth as silk (with only a very light finish, if any), tuning is what allows you to get the maximum height and stability in the hover.

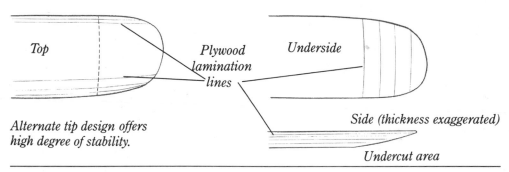

Top

Plywood
lamination
lines

Underside

Side (thickness exaggerated)

*Alternate tip design offers
high degree of stability.*

Undercut area

# TUNING THE MTA

There are as many ways to tune an MTA as there are throwers. A lot has to do with the style of throw. Some people throw lead wing and some throw trailing wing. Some throw off the wind as for a normal boomerang, others throw into the wind and still others actually throw *across* the wind.

Basically, you tune the MTA with the elbow area flat and the two wings flexed up much more than for standard boomerangs. This extra flex, or dihedral, gives stability in the hover but it also requires you to launch the boomerang very vertically or even oververtically (that is, tipped slightly toward your head). Also, the launch should be aimed slightly higher than usual. The amount of flex on each wing varies enormously. It's not unusual to see MTA boomerangs with the lead wing bent up 3½" at the tip and the trailing wing bent up 2" at the tip. It is also common to see some "wash-out" twist put into the trailing wing. This is nothing more than twisting the wingtip so the trailing edge is actually slightly higher than the leading edge when viewed from the end. It is believed that this tuning lets the boomerang spin more freely and results in a longer hover, or "hang time."

# WEIGHTING THE MTA

Weighting is another controversial subject with MTA boomerangs. Most people agree that you need to weight the tips (as shown in diagram 27) to give more spin; however, some add additional weights (grouped on either side of the elbow or just off the elbow on the trailing wing alone) for increased stability.

Whatever tuning or weighting techniques you use, this is perhaps the most difficult boomerang to fly. Practice throwing at about half power to develop your form.

# BIRDS AND BOOMERANGS

One afternoon, while he was throwing a six-bladed pinwheel boomerang in Sacramento, California, aerospace engineer Ted Bailey heard a whooshing noise and saw something large coming right at him just as he was about to make a catch. It was an eagle. "The bird came to rest 10 feet away on the grass," says Bailey. "I was a bit scared and didn't know what to do, so I just stood still." As the two eyeballed each other, people came running toward them. When the first man got within 50 feet, he grasped a long leather cord attached to the eagle's leg, approached the bird and coaxed it to fly onto his fist. It turned out that the zoo-born golden eagle was being trained to fly and hunt, preparatory to its release in the wild. To this day, Bailey wonders whether the big attraction was himself or the six-bladed pinwheel.

Dan Lady of Bristol, Tennessee, reports an interesting brush with a bird after looping his boomerang through a stand of tall trees. He was on his way to retrieve it from the adjacent field when a hawk materialized and dropped onto the 'rang. "The hawk finally realized it wasn't a wounded dove," says Lady, "so he flew off again." As an afterthought, Lady offers: "I'm glad the hawk wasn't a woodpecker."

*Diagram 28. Mini-rang. (⅛" or 3mm plywood)*

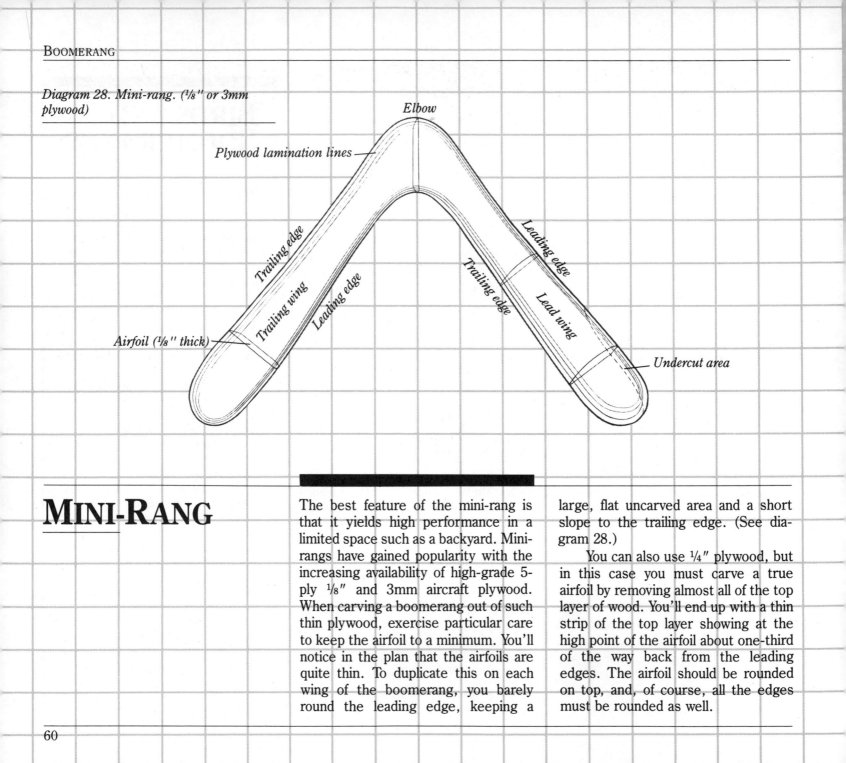

# MINI-RANG

The best feature of the mini-rang is that it yields high performance in a limited space such as a backyard. Mini-rangs have gained popularity with the increasing availability of high-grade 5-ply ⅛" and 3mm aircraft plywood. When carving a boomerang out of such thin plywood, exercise particular care to keep the airfoil to a minimum. You'll notice in the plan that the airfoils are quite thin. To duplicate this on each wing of the boomerang, you barely round the leading edge, keeping a large, flat uncarved area and a short slope to the trailing edge. (See diagram 28.)

You can also use ¼" plywood, but in this case you must carve a true airfoil by removing almost all of the top layer of wood. You'll end up with a thin strip of the top layer showing at the high point of the airfoil about one-third of the way back from the leading edges. The airfoil should be rounded on top, and, of course, all the edges must be rounded as well.

# LORIN HAWES

## An Expatriate Who Became a Boomerang Master

American-born Lorin Hawes, who happily describes his career as "evolution in reverse," earned a doctoral degree in chemistry and worked as an atomic weapons research specialist at Los Alamos, New Mexico, before migrating to Australia in 1956 in search of the better life. While exploring the continent as he awaited an academic appointment, Hawes learned how to make and throw boomerangs—and a second career opened for him.

"I had arrived on the Capricorn Coast in Queensland and set up camp on a beach between Yeppoon and Emu Park: the beach virtually disappeared at high tide, but at low tide it was about half a mile wide—it seemed an ideal place to throw boomerangs. I had acquired a collection of fairly useless artifacts, each one hurtling through the air differently and none returning to me unless lofted into a breeze that would blow it back. Having plenty of time on my hands, I bought a piece of ³⁄₈″ marine plywood and, with a picnic table for a workbench, a hacksaw blade and a pocket knife, a boomerang emerged after two days.

"Its size and shape were based on my observations of the flight characteristics of the ones I had been trying to throw plus my desire to increase the active participation of the boomerang in its own return: I wanted to free it from its dependence upon a breeze to return. The result was about 17 inches long and weighed about three ounces. It was a thicker, yet lighter boomerang than its predecessors and very much livelier in turning around in the air.

"Whenever I took my boomerang with me on picnics, I noticed that people who watched my throwing became interested and wanted one for themselves. Eventually I decided to make a few to sell, and soon I was making about a thousand or so a month. A plastic version that I designed for the Wham-O company in the U.S. helped spread the sport internationally. A short time later I started a tourist attraction in Queensland, which was to become the largest boomerang enterprise in the world."

Hawes and family had settled in the hills behind the Gold Coast, their large tract abounding with giant eucalyptus trees populated by wild koalas. Here they established a nature preserve with kangaroos, ran a riding studio and manufactured boomerangs. Hawes concentrated on the original M17 ("M" for mail order and "17" for length in inches). In a country where all too many of the souvenir boomerangs sold to tourists didn't work at all, his design became a saving grace.

Today, having sold his property after its value soared when the Gold Coast became Australia's Miami Beach, Hawes lives in contented retirement nearby—still crafting boomerangs, but this time collector's items of hardwoods such as Silky Oak and Huon Pine.

AUSTRALIAN NEWS AND INFORMATION BUREAU

# WEIRD SHAPES

**A**s you can see from the pictures, boomerangs can be made in almost any shape imaginable—including that of just about any letter in the alphabet. Few other sports can boast so much freedom in equipment design. While competitions are usually limited to two-bladers, boomeranging is primarily an individual sport. Just as you develop your own throwing style, you can develop your own boomerangs and create a whole new set of games.

CHUCK CARLTON

Models (with designers) from Ben Ruhe's collection: 1) Y- or i-rang (Lesta Bertoia); 2) Straight razor (Rusty Harding); 3) Bobby pin (Bob Foresi); 4) Kangaroo (Dennis Maxwell); 5) Woman (George Reitbauer); 6)Tomahawk (Rusty Harding); 7)A-rang (Lesta Bertoia); 8) Catamarang (Robert Leckie); 9) Gull (Duncan MacLennan); 10) F-rang (Lesta Bertoia); 11) Modified V-rang (Peter Ruhf); 12) E-rang (Lesta Bertoia); 13) R-rang (Flying Trees: Mike Forrester and Ron Tamblyn); 14) M- and W-rang (Flying Trees).

# REPAIRS

When plywood comes into play, breakage is a factor that even expert boomerang throwers have to contend with. Gusty winds can nudge the best of tosses into crash-landings. If your boomerang cracks or breaks, don't despair: at-home repairs are easy, and you may wind up with a stick that performs as well as it always did—or, if you're lucky, even better than before.

## CRACKS

Of the two wounds, cracking is more common but harder to cure. Don't complete the break, since the plies that remain lend strength and serve to line up the boomerang for repair work. If the crack is small, open it up with a toothpick or small nail. Smear on glue, pushing it in for penetration, and wipe off the excess. Slow-drying epoxy is the best glue to use, with good-quality resorcinol wood glue providing an excellent alternative; both are available at hardware stores. Wrap waxed paper around the glued area and, using two pieces of scrap wood, place a splint over the entire section. When the glue has dried, remove splint and waxed paper, sand off any excess glue, and repaint or revarnish to repel moisture.

## BREAKS

If a bad landing or other mishap produces a complete break, glue the two

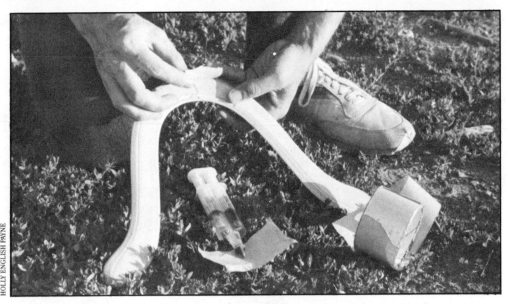

HOLLY ENGLISH PAYNE

*Emergency repairs: the two wings are lined up perfectly before gluing and taping.*

pieces together according to the procedure described above. Take great care to match the pieces perfectly and to avoid either upward or downward warp. When the glue has set in, sand off the excess and repaint or revarnish.

After either type of repair, if appearance isn't crucial, some tape can be wrapped around the damaged area for added strength. One-inch, lightweight fiberglass reinforced strapping tape, available at stationery and hardware stores, is exceptionally effective when wrapped crisscross; a good alternative is aluminum duct tape (*not* regular duct tape, which tends to become gummy under a hot sun). Don't overdo it, though, because too much tape adds weight and changes the boomerang's aerodynamics.

If the splintering or fracture occurs while you're competing or you otherwise need a really quick repair, smear five-minute epoxy on the crack or break, line up the boomerang with great precision to avoid bowing, wipe off the excess glue, and allow the glue to set for 15 minutes. After the set occurs, sand the area smooth, wipe off dust, and wrap stainless-steel tape (available at auto parts stores) over the break. Then smear more glue over the tape. Let dry, then sand down again. The boomerang is ready to throw. If your magic stick is by now rather ugly, think of its cast as a badge of honor.

# BUYING BOOMERANGS

If you're in the market for a boomerang, the most important piece of advice is: *Know your source*. While commercial boomerangs found in sporting goods stores or tourist outlets can be true returners, many are not. Your best option is to purchase by mail order. The United States Boomerang Association (see Appendix for more details) has a newsletter that lists some reputable boomerang manufacturers that sell via mail order.

When assessing the merits of a particular boomerang, keep the following in mind:
● Does the boomerang have anything resembling an airfoil? Are the edges well rounded and well crafted?
● How much does it weigh? Most commercial boomerangs are too heavy to be fun to catch. Beginners should focus on lighter-weight 'rangs like the Darnell that comes with this book.
● Is it warped or twisted? There's no point starting out with one that's way out of whack (even though *you* now know how to fix such problems).

Some boomerangs are expensive yet worth it; others are not. Until you've developed your throwing technique, stay with the medium-priced models ($5 to $15). As you start to appreciate more sophisticated designs and materials, you can begin a boomerang collection. Of course, fine workmanship, inlays and decoration are worthy of a higher price, but this doesn't mean the boomerang will fly any better.

# SOUND-AND-LIGHT SHOW

Throwing a boomerang that whistles in flight adds a nice aural dimension to the sport. Simply drill a hole in one wing or both, down toward the tip but not far enough to interfere with the grip (the angle should be about 30° toward the leading edge). Push an empty .22-caliber rifle shell through the hole, letting the open end of the cartridge protrude from the curved topside of the wing.

If you want to throw your boomerang at night, when the parks are empty and the wind is down, adding light is an easy step. Cyalume, a safe cold-light chemical widely used for Halloween decorations, is quickly adaptable to light boomerangs. You'll need two capsules, each measuring $5/16''$ by $2^7/8''$; if Cyalume (also marketed as Nightstick and Lightstick) is not available in this size at your local hardware or novelty shop, you can purchase it by mail order from Kite Site, 3101 M Street, Washington, D.C. 20007.

Choose a boomerang from your kit that is at least $1/4''$ thick, pick a point midway up one wing from tip to elbow, and rout out a $5/16''$ by 3" slot a third of the way back from and parallel to the leading edge. This is the spot where the chord is thickest. Drill a slot in the

*Slots and Cyalume capsules transform boomerangs into night-rangs.*

CHUCK CARLTON

other arm using the same formula. Now activate the two Cyalume capsules by bending the tubes according to the instructions on the packet. Insert them into the slots and secure with clear strapping tape. Your boomerang will glow brightly for hours.

When you're finished throwing, or if you want to transfer the tubes to another boomerang, peel off the tape and pop the capsules out of their slots. If the chemical is still glowing, place the capsules in a refrigerator freezer to halt the chemical reaction (they'll keep up to a week or so). To reactivate them, just remove them from the freezer and warm them in the palm of your hand until the glow resumes. Used this way, the capsules will yield several hours of tossing over the course of two or three nights.

GEORGE LEAVENS

*George Leavens' boomerang lights up the night sky. (See page 25 for more details.)*

> **❝**Boomeranging is most intriguing. Somewhere between an art and a sport, it has the quality of being completely serious and being total foolery. It abounds with paradoxes . . . it is the sport of poets.**❞**
>
> —*T. W. Smith, Oregon electronics specialist and poet*

# GAMES AND COMPETITIONS

# THE BOOMERANG SCENE

*Ben Ruhe catching in front of the Washington Monument.*

O DD THOUGH IT MAY SEEM, boomeranging as a contemporary sport got its start through educational workshops of the Smithsonian Institution in Washington, D.C. Sparked by a desire to bring more people to the National Mall and based on boomerang collections in the Smithsonian's National Air and Space Museum and National Museum of Natural History, the workshops were conceived (partly out of fun) by staff member Ben Ruhe and first held in the spring of 1969. When they attracted 600 registrants in the first two days, it was clear that a wellspring of interest had been tapped. Smithsonian staff decided to add a small, casual competition to its classes, and boomerang throwing as a new-age American sport was born.

The classes and the tournament were repeated the following year and each spring thereafter. Word got around that this was a sport for the venturesome, and participants arrived from around the country. The tournament, meanwhile, was kept lighthearted and fun. Awards included the General Douglas MacArthur "I Shall Return" Award and the "I-Made-It-Myself Prettiest Boomerang" Award.

WIDE WORLD PHOTOS

*The winner is hoisted in triumph.*

Tourists, too, were drawn to the flings on the Mall in Washington. Seeing boomerangs fly through the sky, one Australian raced over and demanded to know what was going on. When told a boomerang tournament was being held, he shrugged and muttered: "Mad Yanks!" On another occasion, writer J. Timberlake Gibson, who witnessed the activities, termed the competition the next best thing to Washington's singing dog contest.

With each year, the number of entrants swelled and the level of expertise increased. To cope, events were speeded up and new, more difficult competitions involving simultaneous launching were devised. This kept both audiences and television crews absorbed. With success came sponsorship by Australian government agencies, by QANTAS, the Aussie national airline promoting tourism to the Antipodes, and by companies distributing Australian beer in the United States. A national association representing the mail-order industry contributed its own "Many Happy Returns" Award.

Competitions tested a variety of skills and required an arsenal of boomerangs. There was Maximum Time Aloft, Long Distance, Accuracy, Doubling and Juggling. World records were established, and pro-throwers now vied to set marks and get their names in *The Guinness Book of World Records*. From a quirky, solitary, individualistic sport, boomeranging had come a long way.

Liking what they saw, out-of-town visitors took the word home with them and organized their own boomerang clubs and annual corroborees, sometimes with very different rules. Names like the Free Throwers' Boomerang Society, the Talla-Aussie Boomerang Association and the Déjà Vu Aerodynamics Club cropped up in towns across America.

In October 1979 the United States Boomerang Association was established so that American records would be recognized by Guinness. The USBA took over the Nationals and began moving them around the country, first to Virginia, then to Ohio and California. Meanwhile, in sore need of a trip to Australia, Ben Ruhe and his colleague Ali Fujino from Seattle organized a U.S. team to travel Down Under and challenge the Aussies on their home ground. To the surprise of many, not excluding the cocky Yanks, the visitors swept a test series of three matches and brought home the Boomerang Cup. Press reaction Down Under reflected national consternation: "We should hang our heads in shame," lamented the Sydney *Daily Telegraph* after the losses. "Boomerangs? They were invented here. It's enough to make any self-respecting Aussie go bush."

Boomerang clubs soon sprang up all over Europe: some with classic names like the Deutcher Bumerang Club; others a little more esoteric, like the Society for the Promotion and Avoidance of Boomerangs started by British sailplane pilot Dr. Brennig James. The Japanese also became interested. They organized a national federation and imported some Australian throwers to show them the fine points.

At the grass-roots level in the United States, kids are also becoming intrigued by the art and science of boomeranging. A number of them are

HOLLY ENGLISH PAYNE

*The U.S. team competing on its homeground against the Aussies in 1984.*

# ALI FUJINO

## An Organizational Dynamo

JOHN HOLMBERG

**A**mong the many women drawn to the sport of boomeranging, Ali Fujino of Seattle stands out as a model of athletic prowess and leadership ability.

Ali was raised as something of a tomboy by a baseball-playing father. "I'm from a California family," she says, "and we were taught to throw anything that wasn't attached to the ground." After a stint at the Smithsonian Institution, where she discovered boomerangs through the annual workshops, she took two university degrees in the Northwest. Reporting to the University of Washington medical clinic with an injury, she was quizzed by the attending physician, Dr. Steve Miller, about the painted sticks poking out of her bag. Within days, the two were out chucking 'rangs (Miller had been a football quarterback in college and was an adept thrower), and the friendship blossomed into marriage.

Expert not only in organizational work but also in attracting sponsors and raising money, Ali put together the American team's tour of Australia in 1981 and the return visit to the United States by the Aussies in 1984. Financed by the mail-order clothing firm Lands' End, she brought Aussie champ Bob Burwell and Australian super-tot Baby Ben Loveland to the States for demonstration tours in 1982 and 1983, respectively. She also served two terms as president of the United States Boomerang Association, during which she was instrumental in obtaining nonprofit status for the infant organization, codifying national competition rules, setting up an extensive publications program and archives, and bolstering membership. Most important, she made the association national in fact as well as name by moving the annual American championship tournament away from the East Coast to Ohio, then California, with Georgia next in line and Texas at the ready.

Meanwhile, Ali was making her competitive mark. During the 1981 U.S. team tour of Australia, she was a top scorer in the tournament at Brisbane—besting, among others, her husband, who was also a team member. In the 1983 national championship, she became the first woman ever to win a national singles title in the sport anywhere in the world by defeating a visiting Australian thrower in a playoff for the Accuracy title.

An inveterate traveler, Ali has pitched boomerangs around the world. In Nepal she taught a young boy how to throw, and he taught four others ("I had myself a team," Ali says). In India she threw beside the Taj Mahal. In Bali she became a local celebrity ("I could have run for office and won"). During a Peace Corps posting to Honduras, she started a small cottage industry by getting prison inmates interested in making boomerangs for sale.

As to what the sport means to her: "I like being able to compete with other people without being really competitive-minded. Boomerang throwing gives me a sense of mystical pleasure. It's a thinking sport."

apprenticing themselves to master boomerang craftsmen, and some have written serious research papers on boomerangs to help them gain admittance to prestigious universities.

Declaring they wouldn't be welcome to come home if they failed to win this time, a band of determined Aussies came to the United States in 1984 to avenge lost honor. And in a three-match series they did just that, winning two of three matches and recapturing the Lands' End Boomerang Cup. Windy conditions in the first and third throws produced some Yankee ingenuity. U.S. team member Eric Darnell, then a windmill designer, attached a spoiler-like strip on his 'rangs to create drag and prevent them from being blown away. The "wind keel," a play on the controversial "winged keel" used by Australia to win the America's Cup in yachting, accounted for several good scores and lots of jokes. There's talk of a Yankee comeback. Of course, the series will have to take place Down Under because the Australians, like their boomerangs, found a way to return home.

The sport of boomeranging received a giant boost from an unexpected quarter in the summer of 1985. Slow to join the United States and Australia in appreciating the boomerang, Europe surged ahead of both continents with an imaginative $130,000, two-week promotion called the Tour du Boomerang. The tour, organized by

PAUL ZANETTI, *SYDNEY DAILY TELEGRAPH*

two young French business school graduates looking for a promotional event they could call their own, began in Paris with the first annual World Master's Cup tournament sponsored mainly by Hollywood Chewing Gum (General Foods). The invitational was contested by two Aussies, four Americans and six Europeans. Three events common to the three continents, Fast-Catch, Consecutive Catch ("Suicide") and Distance, were the nucleus events. Added were Doubling (from the U.S.), Australian Round (Australia) and Endurance, or Five-Minute Fast

*The Aussie team takes home the Boomerang Cup in 1984.*

HOLLY ENGLISH PAYNE

Catch (Europe). For fairness, each player dropped the score for his poorest event. The location, beside the Seine, was the perfect place to

*Poster advertising the 1985 French games.*

boomerang—fencing, bleachers, windscreen, advertising banners, sound stage, two tents and thousands of spectators, many of them clearly bemused by this new sport.

Eric Darnell took two firsts and a second in the first four events to establish a commanding lead early on. But a playoff in one event, participation in a midafternoon demonstration by the Americans and the hours of competition wore him down while Chet Snouffer, the younger Ohio gymnast, came on strong. Winning a second and two thirds in the initial going, Snouffer took firsts in the final two events to sweep past Darnell and take the championship. With his final foot catch in Consecutive Catch, the last grab of the long day, he became "champion du monde." Third place went to the cannon-armed English teenager David Schummy and fourth to Christophe

Bertrand of France. The tournament was topped off by a night demonstration by the Yankees using boomerangs lit by cold-light chemicals, as a crowd of hundreds of distinguished invited guests watched.

Vitesse ("speed"), the sponsoring French organization, then took the four Americans on a lightning tour of nine beach resorts on the Mediterranean, Atlantic and Channel coasts. Barnaby Ruhe and Peter Ruhf, the two other Americans, were joined by Ben Ruhe as captain and coach. The throwers did three shows daily and some night throws before crowds that often numbered in the thousands. Boomeranging achieved high visibility in some of the most prestigious resorts in France, and free lessons for all comers further spread the word. Said the pleased organizers: "We're going to do it again—*much* bigger!"

As the first international match ever to involve more than two countries, the World Master's Cup appropriately spawned an *ad hoc* international organization to grapple with codifying the various competitions and rules used on three continents as well as setting up an international rating system for players. It is expected that Asia, with representation by Japan, will join the new federation, with Africa and South America participating in due course.

*Every catch counts in competition.*

# WARMING UP

It's wise to warm up before you start throwing boomerangs, in order to prevent muscle pull. The cooler the weather, the more vital are such preliminaries. Stretch out all your muscles, particularly your arms and shoulders. Then whirl your throwing arm around windmill-style, simulate some throws, bend at the waist, and jog in place to limber up. Begin throwing moderately with a lightweight boomerang and use a pinch grip, which is easier on your wrist and elbow. After five minutes or so, you should be sufficiently warmed up and able to let 'em rip.

# GENERAL RULES FOR GAMES AND COMPETITIONS

**1** Meters are used as the standard form of measurement in boomerang throwing because the sport is played in many parts of the world. For easier comprehension, equivalent measurements in yards can be used (one meter equals 39.37 inches, or a little more than one yard).

**2** Contestants are permitted to practice in a warm-up area before competing. To keep up the pace once the competition starts, participants are ordinarily not permitted a test, or "sighter," throw.

**3** Boomerangs must be of the traditional two-armed variety unless a specific event calls for a multiblader.

**4** Decide on the throwing order by asking players to volunteer or draw straws. Left-handers throw at a different angle to the wind than do right-handers and should therefore be grouped together.

**5** Throws must be judged authentic boomerang throws.

**6** Each throw must be made within 20 seconds after the player has taken position, unless the judge permits more time.

**7** Each player is allotted a set number of throws (usually made alternately with other players). This constitutes his round. Generally, his score is the sum of the points he accumulates from each of the throws in the round unless, as in MTA, his best single effort is what is counted. Sometimes two or three rounds make up a game. In those games where players launch in turn, the sequence is speeded up if contestants break into smaller groups (of two or three people) and alternate throws within each group.

**8** Clearly illegal strategies, such as tying thread between wingtips to aid in catching, are barred.

**9** Catches should be as clean as possible, although body-assisted catches are legal. The judge decides. A catch executed as the boomerang touches the ground on return is scored legal if one hand is *under* the 'rang.

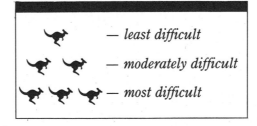

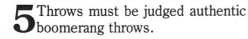 — *least difficult*

— *moderately difficult*

— *most difficult*

VINCE DE WITT, *DAILY HAMPSHIRE GAZETTE*

# ACCURACY

The game of Accuracy is as old as the boomerang itself. A nineteenth-century explorer described Australian Aborigines playing a sophisticated version of this game, lending further support to the role of the boomerang as an instrument of sport in the traditional Aboriginal culture.

A series of 6 concentric circles is laid on the ground. The inner circle, which functions both as the throwing circle and as the bull's-eye, measures 2 meters in radius. Each larger circle increases in radius by 2 meters up until the fifth circle, which has a radius of 10 meters. The sixth and final circle has a 20-meter radius and forms the game's outer limit; that is, throws must travel outward that minimum distance.

## PLAYERS
Two or more

## OFFICIALS
A judge to monitor launches and score returns; a linesman to monitor throwing distances

## OBJECT
To launch a boomerang from the inner circle and make it return to the circle for a bull's-eye.

*Scoring a bull's-eye.*

HOLLY ENGLISH PAYNE

## SCORING
The player who amasses the highest number of points wins. A bull's-eye scores 10 points. If the boomerang comes to rest in the next circle, 8 points are awarded. The progression outward is 6, 4 and 2. If the 'rang is lying across one of the lines, split the difference; in other words, if it's touching the line that delineates the bull's-eye, 9 points are awarded.

## PLAY
Each player, throwing in turn, gets one "sighter" (or practice) throw and three additional throws. The sighter throw can count toward the score or not, at the option of the player; if it counts, two (not three) more throws are granted. A throw is disqualified if the boomerang fails to fly out at least 20 meters or if the player touches the 'rang before it comes to rest on the ground.

## STRATEGY
Since your aim is to throw the boomerang low to the ground and bring it barely back to the bull's-eye, try using a clunky boomerang that won't be pushed around by the wind.

## OTHER DIMENSIONS
Instead of laying out concentric circles, you can use a large, deep-sided bowl, plastic washtub or children's wading pool as the marker. Here the object is to launch the boomerang so that it lands inside the receptacle. In this version only, players are allowed to slap the 'rangs on their return flight in order to guide their landing.

Accuracy can also be played indoors using cardboard or styrofoam four-bladed boomerangs. Players sit around a coffee table, which functions as the throwing marker. The winner is the first person to bring his 'rang back to land on the table.

Another version of Accuracy is played blindfolded. Each player is first allowed to get into his throwing position before being blindfolded. Since boomerang throwing relies so much on eyesight, this version drastically changes the dynamics of the game by forcing players to rely on their other senses plus memory.

# POSITION

Eric Darnell invented and named this game in 1976 in response to a strong Pennsylvania wind that was posing a challenge to a group of throwers.

## OBJECT

To end up as the closest player to the throwing marker following the third and final throw. Position after the first two launches does not matter.

## SCORING

The player closest to the marker after the third round of throws is the winner.

## PLAY

Players launch simultaneously from the marker. Those who catch their boomerangs will make their second launch from that point; those who fail to catch go to their boomerangs, pick them up and then take three *large* penalty steps away from the marker for the second launch. Second throws are now made, and the cycle is repeated. If the player catches, he stays put where the catch occurred; if not, he goes to the dropped boomerang and paces off three large penalty steps away from the marker to establish his new launching spot. The third and final round is the crucial one. With the object of the game being to catch as close as possible to the marker, the player will often be confronted with the need to make a thoroughly bad throw to achieve a good result. Remember, whoever fails to catch on the third throw must take the three penalty steps away from the marker. A best-two-of-three or best-three-of-five series can be run off to determine the grand champion.

## STRATEGY

Position is the name of this game, in more ways than one. While catching helps greatly, it's perfectly possible to win the competition despite three drops. Focus on being in the correct place to make the third throw and then executing it well. Note, however, that players should agree to rule out "throwaways"—purposeful tosses into the ground. Each throw must be a genuine launch with the boomerang arcing around in normal fashion. Leaping catches, as in Out-Back, can improve your spot on the field since your score is determined not by where the catch occurs but by where your foot touches the ground. More important is reading the wind: if it's blowing a bit, you want to take advantage by being upwind for the last toss.

*The game of Position requires simultaneous launches to ensure that everyone deals with the same wind.*

HOLLY ENGLISH PAYNE

# STORING AND CARRYING BOOMERANGS

To prevent warping, boomerangs are best stored upright and should be kept dry. Ideal for both is a cardboard accordion file with a dozen or more pockets. Put socks over any boomerangs that are finely decorated in order to protect the finish. Place the file in a weatherproof shoulder bag, fill with 'rangs and you have the ultimate in good storage, portability and accessibility.

CHUCK CARLTON

HOLLY ENGLISH PAYNE

*Hustling to the marker for a game-winning catch.*

# OUT-BACK

The name of this game derives from the boomerang's flight path—out and back—and is not to be confused with Australia's wide-open spaces called the Outback. Invented by American Peter Ruhf, the game of Out-Back was first played on a farm belonging to writers George and Helen Papashvily in Bucks County, Pennsylvania.

## PLAYERS
Two or more

## OBJECT
To launch a boomerang from a marker and *catch* it on or as close as possible to the same marker.

## SCORING
Three points for touching the boomerang anywhere in the field on its return, 5 points for a catch anywhere, 7 points for touching the 'rang while your foot is on the throwing marker, and a grand-slam 10 points for catching it with your foot on the marker.

## PLAY
Each player throws in turn. Three or five throws constitute a round. High-point scorer wins; to determine a grand champion, a best-two-of-three or best-three-of-five series is played.

## STRATEGY
Going to lengths, literally, to make the catch is what Out-Back is all about. Pretend you're a first baseman in baseball and, with your toe on the marker, stretch way out to grab the boomerang as it drops down several feet away from you. Your score is determined by where your foot touches. Tall players definitely have an advantage here. An alternative strategy is flashier but risky: if the boomerang is hovering down several feet from the marker, you can make a big leap toward home base, attempting to catch the 'rang in midair and then landing on the marker for maximum points. It's where the foot lands that determines your score.

# BEN LOVELAND

## *Aussie Super-Tot*

At the age of 29 months, Baby Ben Loveland defeated a field of several dozen boomerangers to win the Australian junior Accuracy championship—and became probably the youngest national champion in the history of sports. His feat drew worldwide media attention and earned him a promotional tour of the United States, as well as an appearance in a Japanese film on super-achieving children.

Grandson of Bunny Read, a boomerang manufacturer and demonstration thrower in Wycheproof, Victoria, Baby Ben virtually teethed on boomerangs. "I made him his first 'rang after he was born," says Read, "and as a toddler he'd crawl around the house with it in his hand. He even preferred it to his rattle. I used to hold him in my arms when I threw boomerangs outside and he'd say, 'More, 'Pa! More, 'Pa!' He got his first boomerang to return at the age of 18 months."

The last thrower of Ben's size to come this way was the feral child who tossed a lethal boomerang in the Australian movie *Road Warriors*. Ben's visit to the United States, in the summer of 1983, was a far happier occasion. Standing three-foot-three and weighing in at 38 pounds, the barnstorming little blond wowed the crowds at an Oakland A's baseball game, at the Seattle Museum of Flight and at the corporate home of Lands' End, the Wisconsin mail-order firm that sponsored his tour. When a nine-year-old asked him for his autograph in Portland, Oregon, where he gave lessons, Ben announced: "I can't write." In Washington, D.C., for the U.S. Nationals, he seemed to draw more newspaper ink than a concurrently visiting Australian dignitary.

Out in the field, Ben and Bunny Read were a team. The grandfather coached him on his aim, and with his ferocious right arm he would wing his boomerang out 20 yards and bring it right back. In turn Baby Ben lent vocal support to his grandfather's 50-yard pitches. A perfect toss prompted the exclamation "Rippa!" When not playing with his "boomies," Ben turned his attention to the many American gifts he received: a sheriff's badge, stuffed animals, a whistle. Racing cars were a favorite—"fasties," he called them.

Because his grandson was so young, Bunny Read predicted that Ben would remember nothing of his whirlwind trip. Contemporary technology permits otherwise. Today, back home and enrolled in nursery school, Baby Ben spends evenings watching television. His favorite program: a video cassette of himself in action during his triumphant American tour.

# CONSECUTIVE CATCH ("SUICIDE")

With several of his colleagues, Smithsonian Institution tournament organizer Ben Ruhe invented this game in the early 1970s. Developed to cope with the ever-increasing number of tournament entrants, it has been nicknamed "Suicide" because of the chaos that ensues when up to a hundred players launch their boomerangs simultaneously and then must position themselves to catch their own sticks without getting "attacked" by those of other players. The competition presents a stunning spectacle as dozens of boomerangs whine, whiz and whirl through the sky and players weave among each other in what appears to be some strange ritualistic dance. In practice, "Suicide" sorts itself out more easily than spectators assume from all the hurly-burly, so progressively more difficult catches were added during the 1977 Smithsonian Institution boomerang fling. Finalists Richard Harrison of Monroe, Louisiana, and Dr. Larry Ruhf of Belchertown, Massachusetts, staged a cliff-hanger for the championship (finally won by Harrison) that had spectators standing on chairs and cheering wildly. Their long duel marked the beginning of boomerang throwing as a tournament sport in the United States.

## PLAYERS

The more the better

## OFFICIALS

Several needed to judge catches. When there is a large group of players an honor system can be used.

## OBJECT

To make a series of progressively more difficult catches; no drops allowed.

## SCORING

The survivor wins.

## PLAY

Contestants form a line facing the wind, roughly elbow to elbow. On command of a judge, all launch simultaneously. Each player must track his boomerang in the air, avoid other players maneuvering around the field, and snag his own 'rang on its return. The first catch is two-handed; if a player fails to catch, he is eliminated and must leave the playing area. Survivors line up as before and launch on command. This time the boomerang must be caught one-handed. Drop and you're out (this applies to all subsequent rounds). For the third round, survivors relaunch and must catch

*Contestants line up for the simultaneous launch in Consecutive Catch.*

RON STUMPF

with the other hand. The fourth catch must be two-handed, behind the back. The fifth, two-handed, under the leg. The sixth, if there are still survivors, must be made with the feet. In case of a tie, a repeat round can be ordered or the surviving players can be declared joint champions. If there are no winners in any given round, that round is repeated.

## STRATEGY

Use a lightweight boomerang that yields a nice hover to allow you to position yourself well for each catch.

While not as dangerous as its name implies, "Suicide" calls for steely concentration and should be played only by relatively experienced throwers. Midair collisions of boomerangs do occur, but you can cut the odds by positioning yourself at or close to the end of the line. Above all, Consecutive Catch calls for determination.

## OTHER DIMENSIONS

This game can, of course, be simplified to accommodate players who are not adept at trick catches. In the modified version, players launch simultaneously and catch two-handed in successive rounds until there is a sole survivor. "Suicide" also makes an entertaining game for two or possibly three players tossing cardboard 'rangs indoors.

# THE WILLIAM TELL STUNT

**A**s in all sports, there are some feats in boomeranging that are reserved only for the very few. The William Tell stunt is one of these and should never be attempted by the readers of this book or even by experienced players. In fact, only a handful of experts can perform this trick, which is really much more fun to watch than perform.

In the boomerang version of the Swiss legend, instead of the father shooting an apple off his son's head with bow and arrow, the thrower himself dons the apple, launches a boomerang and on the return permits it to slice the apple off his own head.

Barnaby Ruhe of New York City and eastern Pennsylvania (he actually seems to live in a truck) conceived the stunt and performed it on a 1982 *That's Incredible* program for millions of television viewers. Now several other throwers, jealous of all this media attention, have learned "William Tell"—including Eric Darnell, Peter Ruhf and Chet Snouffer.

The stunt actually *is* dangerous, requiring a boomerang heavy enough to slice off the apple and allowing no room for misjudgment. Furthermore, no matter how accurate the player's throw, a last-second gust of wind could cause the boomerang to come in too low. The William Tell stunt is not for the faint-hearted.

*Barnaby Ruhe's headlining William Tell stunt.*

WIDE WORLD PHOTOS

The general idea for the stunt came from a Scottish physicist, Michael Hanson, who visited a Smithsonian tournament in the 1970s and donned a two-foot-high papier-mâché apple he had made for a demo trick. It failed to work for him (the apple fell off after the launch and before the boomerang came back), but onlooker Barnaby Ruhe made a mental note and next year was showing off his version of the trick—using a real apple. He's been doing it ever since and has made front-page news around the world.

HOLLY ENGLISH PAYNE

# DOUBLING

🦘🦘

Inspired by Eric Darnell's stunt of simultaneously launching four natural wood-elbow boomerangs from one hand and catching all four on return, Ben Ruhe added Doubling as an event in the Smithsonian Institution's tournament for 1978. Over the years, progressively more difficult catches have been added until now the game resembles Consecutive Catch with a double-handed twist.

## PLAYERS

Two or more (dozens can compete at one time)

## OFFICIALS

Several needed to judge catches of all the players. Alternatively, pairs of boomerangers can judge each other and report scores to a record keeper.

## OBJECT

To throw two boomerangs at once from the same hand and catch both on their return.

## SCORING

The survivor wins.

## PLAY

Forming a line facing the wind, on command of a judge all players launch two boomerangs simultaneously from one hand. Each must track his own boomerangs in flight, avoid other players and catch both 'rangs on their return. Failing to catch either one ousts the player from the event and he must leave the playing area. Through-out the entire competition, players must retain possession of the first boomerang they catch while making the second grab; the first boomerang can be held in the hand, stowed between the teeth (not a good idea but often done), placed in a pocket or tucked under a belt (the most common strategy). Two-handed sandwich grabs are stipulated for the first round. Survivors of the initial round line up as before for the second round and launch simultaneously on command. This time one-handed catches must be made. If all contestants drop, the round is repeated. A sole survivor is declared the winner; two or more survivors proceed to the third round. This time, the first catch is made one-handed, the second with the other hand. If all contestants drop, the round is repeated; two or more survivors also means that the round is repeated. If two or more make catches on the replay, they can be declared joint champions. Or the judges, in conference, may stipulate a round of still more difficult catches.

## STRATEGY

This event requires "doublers"—two boomerangs that can be gripped together and launched simultaneously, then caught in succession. A variety of combinations will achieve the same result. The first boomerang, the insider, is the key to your success in this competition. You want a boomerang that returns low and fast for a quick catch. Some people use a small lightweight "clunky" boomerang (with poorly carved airfoils) that barely flies; others drill holes in the wings to "spoil" the lift, thereby causing the boomerang to sink quickly; still others use a "fast catch" boomerang. In all these cases, the second boomerang, the outsider, should be a floater that will obediently hover while you catch the first. You can also use a regular boomerang for the insider of the doubling pair and go for a maximum-time-aloft type for the second.

*The grip for the Doubling launch. Holes in the first returner make it come in fast, while the second hovers in more slowly.*

# PINWHEEL POWER

**B**oomerang throwers almost by definition are people with a creative turn of mind. There are loads of tricks out there just waiting to be invented, so why not figure out something for yourself?

Multi-bladers offer some interesting possibilities. Pinwheel throwing, for instance, is a beautiful sight to behold. Assembled with a bolt in the center, the six-bladers can easily be caught spinning on the palm of your hand. The spinning 'rang can then be tossed into the air and caught on your other palm. Showoffs catch the multi-blader spinning on the top of their heads.

*A young thrower performs "pinwheel" magic at the Eighth Annual Boomerang Festival, sponsored by the Smithsonian Resident Associate Program.*

CHESLYE LARSON

LILLIAN M. O'CONNELL, SMITHSONIAN RESIDENT ASSOCIATE PROGRAM

81

# 40-METER ROUND

🦘🦘

This is basically a refinement of the Accuracy game. The rules can be quite complicated, so the simplest version is presented here. The same Accuracy circles are used, but 30-meter, 40-meter and usually 50-meter radius lines are added. Points are awarded separately for distance throwing, accurate returns, and catching; this allows players of differing abilities to compete together with interesting results.

## OFFICIALS
A judge to monitor launches and score returns; several linesmen on each of the 30-meter, 40-meter and 50-meter circles to monitor throwing distances

## OBJECT
To launch a boomerang from the inner circle, have it soar out beyond the 50-meter circle and return for the catch in the center circle. A perfect score would require a player to throw his boomerang out 50 meters (6 points) and catch it (4 points) in the center circle (10 points) for a bull's-eye total of 20 points.

## SCORING
As in Accuracy, the player amassing the most points wins. The Accuracy circles are scored the same, but in addition 2 points are given for a 30-meter throw, 4 points for 40 meters, and 6 points for 50 meters. Also, 4 points are awarded for a catch anywhere inside the 20-meter circle and 2 points are awarded for a catch anywhere outside this circle.

## PLAY
Players are divided into groups of two or three. Players in one group make their throws, then the next group has a go. The members of each group, throwing alternately, get a "sighter" throw and two or three additional throws (depending on whether they opt to keep their "sighter" score). When everyone has had one round of throws, there is a second round usually consisting of the top 10 scorers. This round proceeds like the first, and the best scorer overall wins.

## STRATEGY
It is often wise to use an accurate 30-meter boomerang over a 50-meter 'rang that might be blown off course or fail to make a full return in dead calm. Attempt to make every catch for bonus points.

*Fran Wieckowski stretches for extra points.*

HOLLY ENGLISH PAYNE

# LES AND ARTHUR JANETSKI

## *Octogenarian Wizards*

BENJAMIN RUHE

**A**t an age when many people retire to wheelchairs, Les and Arthur Janetski became national sports figures in Australia. In 1981 the two brothers from Albury captained the only team to defeat the touring American boomerang-throwing squad. In 1985, at the age of 84, Les won an individual championship in Accuracy in the Barooga-Albury Open, defeating an all-star field that included four members of the previous year's Australian national team. Not to be outdone, his kid brother Arthur, 81, threw in the same difficult New South Wales high wind and took second place in the day's most difficult competition: Australian Round, which puts a premium on distance throwing, pinpoint accuracy and adept catching.

Les and Arthur are also renowned for their beautifully crafted boomerangs. Les does the cutting and shaping; Arthur adds the intricate Aborigine-style designs (it takes them each a day's work to make one 'rang). Their sticks are considered by many to be the best-made on the continent. In addition to their impressive decoration they are particularly noted as windcutters—a boon for competition throwing. Among their personal favorites are the Undulating U, a chevron-shaped number with arms curved in squiggles, and the Admiral's Hat, an omega design with flared tips. The latter, when held atop the head, looks like something Admiral Nelson might have worn.

Although Janetski boomerangs are not for sale, the brothers occasionally present them as gifts in exchange for contributions to a small boomerang museum housed in their backyard workshop. The museum contains examples of all the models the Janetskis have constructed over the years plus gift 'rangs and other memorabilia.

Headliner vaudeville performers in the 1920s, when they had a xylophone and soft-shoe dancing routine, the brothers enjoy reminiscing about their involvement in the famous Tivoli circuit in Australia and New Zealand. This career was followed by another as shopkeepers that lasted more than 30 years. In retirement, they came to boomerangs. "We saw a boomerang in a butcher shop here in Albury," Les recalls, "and we got a bit fascinated with it. We went in and bought it. When we got home, we couldn't throw it, couldn't get it to return. We finally learned how to throw by ourselves, and started to make our own boomerangs." They helped organize a local throwing club and have been enthusiastic participants in the sport ever since.

Slender, well-preserved, pink-cheeked men no taller than five-foot-three, the brothers retain a certain show business radiance. On the playing field their faces are customarily wreathed in smiles. Coming off the field, they caper jauntily and click their heels in the air.

# JUGGLING

🪃🪃🪃

During their demonstrations at agricultural fairs in Australia, Brisbane's Bob Burwell and his family developed the art of juggling—throwing and catching two boomerangs alternately, keeping one in the air at all times. A supreme test of eye-hand coordination, body control, stamina and ability to judge the wind while performing under pressure, Juggling was added to the Smithsonian Institution's tournament events in 1978 and has been a tournament mainstay across the United States ever since.

## PLAYERS
Two or more

## OFFICIALS
A judge to supervise the event and a counter to announce the total after each catch

## OBJECT
To make as many consecutive catches as possible during a juggling sequence.

## SCORING
The highest number of juggling catches uninterrupted by a drop wins.

## PLAY
Each player is granted one turn (or perhaps two, depending on the number of competitors). Using two matched "floater" boomerangs, the player throws one, gauges where it will drop down to him, launches the second, catches the first, marks the flight of the second, and relaunches, etc. Catch and launch, catch and launch. If a boomerang is not caught, the skein ends. By preagreement, any thrower who fails to run his total up to five in a row may be given a second chance. This rule takes into account the importance of establishing a rhythm.

## STRATEGY
Use a perfectly matched pair of boomerangs so that they perform identically when thrown in the same manner. "Floaters," or boomerangs with a long hover, are the best because the longer the hover, or "hang time," the more time you have to position yourself for the catch.

You can also tune your matched boomerangs to increase their hovering ability. Leave the lead wing neutral and bend the trailing wing up, starting right near the elbow. (Remember that polypropylene boomerangs can be bent in the field, whereas it's safer to heat plywood boomerangs before tuning. See page 27 for more details.) This bend causes the lead wing to take on more positive incidence (angle of attack) and the trailing wing to take on

*Eric Darnell prepares for the Juggling launch.*

some washout, or negative incidence, allowing it to ride in the slipstream of the lead wing.

Consistent throwing is essential. If your returns range over the field, you'll tire quickly, lose concentration

*This Juggling photograph shows the vertical launch of one boomerang as the second hovers in horizontally for the catch.*

and either make a bad throw or fail to execute the catch. "Floater" boomerangs are easily nudged downwind, so start throwing at the point of the field that is farthest upwind.

With each catch, make sure the boomerang is secure before looking up to locate the one that's still in the air and coming toward you. If the incoming boomerang reaches the highest point of its flight behind your shoulder, it will land behind you; if its highest point is in front of your shoulder, it will land in front of you. Make a mental note of where you need to move in order to catch it, then launch the first one again, taking into account any variations in the wind pattern.

## ANOTHER DIMENSION

An easier version of this game is played indoors with cardboard or styrofoam four-bladers, affording you the opportunity to improve the consistency of your throws without having to take into account the exigencies of the wind. But watch out for furniture!

## WORLD RECORD

Barnaby Ruhe of eastern Pennsylvania scored 161 consecutive catches at a Richmond, Virginia, tournament in August 1984. Ruhe used a pair of medium-size, V-shaped floater boomerangs, with flared wingtips of his own design, named Eurydice and No. 39. He threw nonstop for 20 minutes.

# CATCH AS CAT CAN

**F**risbee-catching dogs are a dime a dozen, but who ever heard of a boomerang-catching cat? Well, Rattie P. Ruhe, jointly owned by Ellen Blue Phillips and Ben Ruhe, taught himself how. Rattie (for his ratlike tail) is a muscular, silver-blue Korat whose parents were brought from Thailand. Observing his master throwing a lightweight cardboard boomerang indoors, Rattie positioned himself under the boomerang, jumped in the air and grasped it between his paws as it hovered down. Congratulated extravagantly, he repeated the feat until the boomerang was mangled. Then he proceeded to chew on it.

When he's in the mood, Rattie will do his stunt for spectators, but he won't perform on command. When a television crew came to film him one day, he resolutely hid behind the plants.

*Rattie P. Ruhe.*

85

# MAXIMUM TIME ALOFT (MTA)

Directly inspired by the Frisbee competition of the same name, MTA was included in the U.S. tournament scene in the late 1970s. To add drama, a catch was made mandatory.

## PLAYERS
Two or more

## OFFICIALS
Two judges to call fair catches and to act also as timers; two stop watches are essential in case of timer malfunction or disparate readings

## OBJECT
To launch a boomerang high in the sky, keep it airborne as long as possible, then catch it on its descent.

## SCORING
The longest time aloft wins.

## PLAY
A *big* field is required, particularly if there is some wind. Players launch in turn and each person is granted five throws per round. The launch spot is not critical as maximum time in the air, not distance covered, is what is being measured. Catches must be made in view of the judges. If a catch is not made, the throw does not count.

## STRATEGY
This event calls for special ultra-light (1/8"-thick) boomerangs, tuned and weighted to maximize their hovering properties. (See pages 58 and 59 for details on how to construct and tune your own.) Because they're so light and can be thrown 100 or so feet off the ground, the wind is a big factor to contend with. If possible, let others go first so you can study where they have to move in order to catch their boomerangs. It helps psychologically to "get on the board," that is, to score a catch with the first or second throw. Then you can uncork behemoth throws to try and better your time. You may also want to delay your catch until your 'rang almost hits the ground. In this instance, you must weigh the possibility of adding a few extra seconds to your time against the odds of successfuly executing a trickier catch.

## OTHER DIMENSIONS
If you have the opportunity to choose the playing field, try to find one where thermals or rising air currents occur. Produced by the sun heating the earth's surface, these factors help a hovering boomerang stay up longer. Grassy areas and concrete lots are two spots where you can find thermals in the heat of the day. Rising air currents

*Larry Ruhf, master MTA thrower, demonstrates the perfect game launch (very high and very vertical) to stabilize the boomerang into a long hover.*

BOB LARAMIE   *TRANSCRIPT TELEGRAM*

also result from the flow of air over an inclined surface, so position yourself on a small elevation.

## WORLD RECORD
Mike Forrester of Wheaton, Maryland, clocked 50.8 seconds aloft with catch at the Eastern Regionals, June 1984, in Bethlehem, Pennsylvania. Forrester used a large, ultra-light, weighted hockey-stick-shaped boomerang designed to autorotate for a long hover. He made the catch almost 100 yards downwind from the launch point. In a practice throw, but under near tournament conditions, Peter Ruhf has scored a 1-minute, 35-second time with catch.

# FAST-CATCH

🦘 🦘 🦘

Invented as a tournament competition in Australia in the late 1970s, Fast-Catch is one of the liveliest of all boomerang events.

## OFFICIALS
Two timers and a linesman to monitor flight distance

## OBJECT
To make five throws and catches as fast as possible.

## SCORING
The player making five catches in the fastest time wins.

## PLAY
Launching in turn from inside a 2-meter-radius throwing circle, each player gets one round of five throws. The boomerang must fly outward a minimum distance of 20 meters and can be caught anywhere on its return. All throws must, however, be made from the launching circle. After the fifth catch, if the player has not caught his boomerang while inside the circle, he must run back to the center in order to end the round. Two failures to catch eliminate the player and no score is given. If a throw does not make the distance, the linesman must signal immediately so the player can take an extra throw. Because of this possibility, a lap timer should be used. Players may also be granted second or third rounds.

*John Flynn shows the form that gained him the Fast-Catch world record.*

FRANCIS V.K. RICHARDS

## STRATEGY
Although any kind of boomerang can be used in Fast-Catch, one that flies low and fast affords a competitive advantage. A simple tuning trick will make your boomerang fly low all the way around back to you: leave the lead wing neutral and bend the trailing wing down a little; this keeps it close to the ground because of the increased resistance of the two wings flying in different planes.

Your goal, through tuning adjustments and deft throwing, is to get the boomerang to come in at chest height. The catch (for a right-hander) is made to the left of the body as you start your pivot to relaunch. A smooth turn-around between catching and launching is what you're aiming for, so be sure to slow down enough to catch your 'rang. Fast-Catch poses a dilemma for the hot-dogger because if he throws a small, slim, weighted boomerang that comes whizzing back, he may drop it and lose crucial time. A slower 'rang may be more effective.

Try and tune and/or weight your boomerang so that it will travel no more than a meter or two over the 20-meter minimum distance. Because distance is so critical, remember also to launch from the edge of circle closest to the direction you're throwing.

## OTHER DIMENSIONS
Turn Fast-Catch on its head and you come up with Endurance, a European invention that tests pacing and stamina, affords fine competition for throwers and is absorbing for spectators. Using basic Fast-Catch rules, Endurance tests how many total catches can be made in five minutes, with the boomerang being launched from a center circle and traveling a minimum distance of 20 meters.

## WORLD RECORD
John Flynn of New London, New Hampshire, has dominated the record book in Fast Catch, establishing the 18.74-second mark for the five throws and catches at the New England Open in August 1985. Flynn also set a new world record for Endurance, scoring 59 catches in five minutes.

# ORGANIZING YOUR OWN TOURNAMENT

Have your day in the sun! Hold your own small tournament and bask in all the attention that it attracts.

## PLANNING

∧ Pick a date when the weather is likely to be warm. The best time of day is late afternoon, when breezes usually abate. Make sure your event doesn't conflict with a rival activity.

*An early Smithsonian Tournament poster suggests ideas for boomerang fliers.*

Establish a rain or wind date in case postponement is necessary.

∧ Allow enough lead time to get organizational work done.

∧ Reserve a flat, grassy field, free of obstructions and at least the size of a soccer field. Check for insurance requirements with the owner of the field.

∧ Don't do everything yourself; secure some volunteer help. Send in the date and location of the event to the secretary of the USBA (see Appendix) so that as many throwers as possible can make plans to participate.

∧ Find sponsors to give cash and prizes in return for publicity. Get a big but inexpensive trophy for the first-place winner and name it after your principal sponsor, or offer a good number of small but interesting prizes. Since boomeranging is closely linked with Australian tourism, inquire at the Australian Consulate or Tourist Commission offices in New York, San Francisco and elsewhere for the names of Australian corporations that offer promotional items at no cost. Consider charging a small entrance fee ($15–$20) to help with expenses.

∧ Let TV and radio stations, magazines (if you have sufficient lead time) and newspapers know about your event by sending out a press release or public service announcement. Offer any media interviewer a lesson in boomerang throwing.

∧ While you can't control advance

## PERSONAL BEST

**I**f you've got the hang of some boomerang games but haven't yet watched or participated in a competition, you can measure your skill against the following standards.

*Intermediate thrower.* Five fast catches: 45 seconds or less. Maximum Time Aloft (MTA) with catch: 15 seconds or more. Juggling: 3 or more consecutive catches. Doubling: both 'rangs must be caught on their return.

*Advanced thrower.* Five fast catches: 35 seconds or less. MTA with catch: 20 seconds or more. Juggling: 5 or more consecutive catches. Doubling: one of the boomerangs is caught with one hand, the other with the second hand.

media coverage, you can ensure that word gets out on your tournament by posting an inexpensive but flashy flier on appropriate bulletin boards, trees, poles, etc. The flier should give details such as eligibility, categories, events, prizes and sponsors. List a source and phone number for more information.

∧ Choose events that are easy to run and that all competitors can grasp quickly. Accuracy, Consecutive Catch, Position and Out-Back are likely choices; if throwers are adept, you can add Maximum Time Aloft, Fast Catch,

Juggling and Doubling. Be inventive—come up with your own games, too.

∧ Decide on what equipment will be needed. A portable, amplified bullhorn is the most useful item, enabling you to maintain control at all times while keeping everyone briefed and interested. A small flag to show wind direction adds color. Stopwatches and a tape measure will be needed, as will Frisbees, paper plates pegged in the ground or bright orange traffic cones for delineating throwing positions. To make circles, one end of a rope measuring the length of each radius is held at the center of the proposed circle while the other end is placed at various points on the perimeter so that lime (if allowed on the field), sawdust or flour can be laid down.

## TOURNAMENT DAY

∧ Appoint a tournament director—yourself?—to oversee operations and to make final decisions. Before the start of the competition, the director should meet with the players and any officials to review the competition rules. A safety officer should also be appointed to enforce the rules for safe throwing (see page 20). One or two judges, as appropriate, are required for each event. These are sometimes players temporarily assigned by the tournament director; that is, players can act as judges when it is not their turn to throw. A judge's role includes: determining what is accepted as a

HOLLY ENGLISH PAYNE

| EVENT | WORLD RECORD | N.Y.C. RECORD |
|---|---|---|
| DISTANCE | A. GERHARDT 123 YDS. (1979) GUINNESS BOOK | |
| FAST CATCH | B. READ 33.00 SEC. (1982) | PETER RUHF 42.95 |
| MAX. TIME | M. FORRESTER 24.41 SEC. (1981) | MIKE FORRESTER 22.43 |

*A blackboard is useful for listing tournament events and records.*

throw and a catch, acting as timer, spotting distance for Accuracy, Fast Catch and 40-Meter Round, and, of course, settling any disagreements within each game. Depending on the size of the event, the roles of timer and linesman can be assigned to different people.

∧ Set up a table for registration and for display of awards. When registering participants, sign them up to a USBA membership (ask the secretary or treasurer for forms). A rollbook is ideal for recording the contestants' names and their scores for each event.

⋏ Establish a warm-up area and permit only registered throwers to use it. You're more likely to have a day of safe throwing if contestants are restricted to the warm-up area and the competition circle. Distinct areas should be established for throwers and spectators, and these should be monitored at all times. If you've arranged to have boomerangs for sale, make it a condition that new purchases are not tested during the tournament. Ask people to wait until after the final event to try them out.

⋏ For each event, points can be awarded on the basis of 10 points for first place, 7 for second, 5 for third, 3 for fourth and 1 for fifth. Or, if there are, say, 10 competitors, first place can be worth 10 points, second 9, third 8, etc. Non-finishers score zero. Ties can be settled by playoffs requiring progressively more difficult catches: one-handed, other-handed, behind-the-back, etc. If time does not permit this, deadlocked players are declared to be tied and the points are split among them; for instance, if two throwers tie for first place, they are both declared winners and the first- and second-place points are divided between them. The next player in line is then awarded third place.

⋏ After the final event, hold an awards ceremony on the field and a party celebrating the fling at a favorite hangout. For the Long Island Invitational at Old Westbury, New York, a table is set up with a vast array of prizes—from six-packs of Australian beer to stuffed koalas and T-shirts. Often boomerang designers will contribute their creations as prizes. Names of contestants are read aloud in order of highest score, with the first-place thrower getting the first choice of prizes, the second-place thrower getting the second choice, and so on. Everyone who entered the competition should get a prize; this encourages newcomers to the sport.

HOLLY ENGLISH PAYNE

# APPENDIX

## I. JOIN THE USBA

The United States Boomerang Association invites you to accept the physical and intellectual challenge of the returning boomerang, "the thinking man's Frisbee." Membership in the USBA provides:

A wide-ranging quarterly newsletter with information on competitions and records, boomerang technology and designs, personalities in the sport around the globe, cartoons and photographs, and much more.

A variety of printed materials such as competition rules, a guide to plywood sources, a list of boomerang makers and distributors, and reprints of technical articles. Videocassettes and films are available on a networking basis.

Free entry in USBA-sponsored tournaments.

Discounts on boomerangs, supplies, publications and wearables advertised in the newsletter.

An opportunity to be a part of and to help shape a growing international sport.

Single memberships, $10; foreign memberships, $20 (includes airmail delivery of newsletter). Family, business and corporate memberships are available. Write to: USBA, Box 2146, Lower Burrell, Pa. 15068.

## II. CLUBS AND ASSOCIATIONS

Algemene Boemerang Organiatie—Holland. Max Hoeben, Rembrandtweg 197, 1181GH Amstelveen, Holland.

Atlanta Boomerang Association. Dr. Brent Russell, 145 Peachtree Park Dr. E-5, Atlanta, Ga. 30309.

Boemerang Vereniging. Ger Schurink, v. Assendelftshof 12, 2312 PJ, Leiden, Holland.

Boomerang Association of Australia. Dianne Jonson, 21 Pleasant Ave. E, Lindfield NSW, Australia.

Boomerang Association of Nigeria. James Ejokwu, Box 4741, Onitsha, Nigeria.

Boomerang Association of Texas. Hugh Vandergrift, 203 Daffodil Dr., Killeen, Tex. 76542.

Boomerang-Club de France. Jacques Thomas, 24 Rue Tronchet, 69006 Lyon, France.

Boomerang Club of Bell Labs. Gar Moy, 20330 Bell Labs, Whippany Rd., Whippany, N.J. 07981.

British Boomerang Society. John Jordan, 9 Bowood Dr., Wolverhampton WV6 9AW, England.

Cleveland Boomerang Club. Dave Boehm, Box 17385, Euclid, Ohio 44117.

Deutscher Bumerang Club. Gunther Veit, Bruckenstrasse 24, 5500 Trier, West Germany.

European Boomerang Federation. Max Hoeben, Rembrandtweg 197, 1181GH Amstelveen, Holland.

Free Throwers' Boomerang Society. Chet Snouffer, 51 Troy Rd., Delaware, Ohio 43015.

Maryland Boomerang Society. Dave Robson, 309 C Burke Ave., Towson, Md. 21204.

Pacific Northwest Boomerang Association. Ali Fujino, 3009 137th Ave. NE, Bellevue, Wash. 98005.

San Diego Boomerang Club. Dan Russell, Box 84895, San Diego, Calif. 92138.

South Florida Boomerang Society. John Saccente, Omni International F-5, 1601 Biscayne Blvd., Miami, Fla. 33132.

South Pacific Boomerang Club. Bill Safer, Tinian School, Marianas Islands.

Svenska Bumerang Sallskapet. Lasse Carenvall, Kastalagatan 6, S-442 36, Kungalv, Sweden.

Swiss Boomerang Club. Nguyen Anh Kim, Burstwiesenstr. 41, 8608 Greifensee, Switzerland.

Talla-Aussie Boomerang Association. Ed Pieratte, Box 6248, Tallahassee, Fla. 32301.

University of California at San Francisco Boomerang Club. Cindy Easton, 1439 35 St., San Francisco, Calif. 94122.

United States Boomerang Association. Ray Rieser, Box 2146, Lower Burrell, Pa. 15068.

# III. SELECTED BIBLIOGRAPHY

Caranvall, Lasse. *Bumerangboken—En Handbok for den nyfikine.* Kungalv, Sweden: 1983. An introduction to the boomerang, by a young Swedish enthusiast.

Cassidy, John. *The Boomerang Book.* Palo Alto, Calif.: Klutz Press, 1985. The skeptic's approach, presented in large format with lots of photos. Working boomerang on cover.

Forsyth, Barrie, ed. Eyre Peninsula Boomerang Society newsletter, 75 Norrie Ave., Wyalla Norrie, Australia.

Hakansson, Carolyn. *Boomerangs.* Reed College dissertation, 1984. A well-reasoned study for the technically minded.

Hall, Steve. "Boom in 'Rangs Launches Old Toy into New Orbit," *Smithsonian Magazine,* June 1984. A lively article that catches the spirit of the boomerang with insight and charm.

Hanson, M. J. *The Boomerang Book.* Harmondsworth, England: Penguin Books, 1974. A Scottish science teacher introduces the boomerang to children. Amply illustrated, with left-handers given as much attention as righties.

Harding, Rusty. *The Boomerang Bible* (in manuscript). An unpublished book by a Tennessee aerodynamicist, aimed at the adept thrower and maker; complex principles explained with clarity.

Hawes, Lorin L. *All About Boomerangs.* Sydney, Australia: Hamlyn Group, 1975. A hard-cover volume by the Queensland master carver. Six pages of color reproductions of Aboriginal and contemporary boomerangs.

Hess, Felix. "The Aerodynamics of Boomerangs," *Scientific American,* November 1968, pp. 124–36. The article that helped launch the current worldwide scientific and sporting interest in the boomerang.

——. *Boomerangs: Aerodynamics and Motion.* Groningen, Holland: privately printed doctoral dissertation, 1975. The Dutch physicist's 555-page thesis: the definitive analysis of the flight of the boomerang.

Hoeben, Max, ed. European Boomerang Federation newsletter, Rembrandtweg 197, 1181GH Amstelveen, Holland.

Jordan, John, ed. British Boomerang Society newsletter, 9 Bowood Dr., Wolverhampton WV6 9AW, England.

Lewis, Murray, ed. Boomerang Assoc. of Australia Bulletin, 7 Shalimar Ct., Vermont, Victoria 3133, Australia.

Mason, Bernard S. *Boomerangs: How to Make and Throw Them.* New York: Dover, 1974. Aimed at children (first printed in 1937). Nicely written and illustrated; an excellent supplement to other books on boomerangs.

Mauro, John. *An Introduction to Boomerangs.* Richmond, Va.: United States Boomerang Association, 1985. A succinct introduction to the boomerang, by the president of the USBA; complete with a valuable section on weighting boomerangs.

Mayhew, H. L., Jr. *The Big Book on Boomerangs.* Columbus, Ohio: Come Back Press, 1982. A wide-ranging compilation of articles, odd facts and photographs.

——. *How to Catch a Boomerang Without a Net.* Columbus, Ohio: Come Back Press, 1983. A sequel to the above, documenting the contemporary boomerang scene with text and more than 100 photos of leading throwers in action.

Pignone, Giacomo. *Boomerang: Fascino di un Arma Preistorica.* Florence, Italy: Editoriale Olimpia, 1980. A study in Italian of both the killer-stick and returning boomerang, with line illustrations and some interesting photos.

Robson, David. *Why Boomerangs Return.* Baltimore, Md.: privately printed, 1977. Exactly why a boomerang boomerangs, by a Baltimore science teacher; includes a first-rate explanation of gyroscopic precession.

Ruhe, Ben. *Boomerang.* Washington, D.C.: Minner Press, 1982. (Originally published by Viking Penguin.) Helped spread the word about the fun of boomeranging around the world. Covers history, physics, construction, throwing, games, records and feats, killer-sticks, and more. Illustrated by Peter Ruhf. "A charming essay in practical anthropology," commented the New York *Times*.

——, ed. *Many Happy Returns: A Quarterly Newsletter on the Art and Sport of Boomeranging*, 1882 Columbia Rd. N.W., Washington, D.C. 20009.

—— and Hawes, Lorin. *The Boomerang*. Washington, D.C.: Smithsonian Institution, 1972. (Revised 1982.) Produced for the Smithsonian Institution workshops; forerunner (in its first of many versions) of the deluge of books on the subject soon to appear in print.

Schurink, Ger. *Boemerangs*. Zutphen, Holland: Thieme and Cie., 1980. Color illustrations and plans for boomerangs make this paperback worth a look no matter what your language. German transl. from the Dutch: *Bumerangs* (Stuttgart, Franchkh'sche Verlagshandlung, 1982).

——, ed. Boemerang Vereniging newsletter, v. Assendelftshof 12, 2312 PJ, Leiden, Holland.

Smith, Herb. *Boomerangs: Making and Throwing Them*. Littlehampton, England: Gemstar Publications, 1975. One of the classics, with nicely drawn plans. The chapter on making and throwing long-range boomerangs is a significant contribution to the sport.

Snouffer, Chet, ed. *The Leading Edge,* Free Throwers' Boomerang Society newsletter, 340 Troy Rd., Delaware, Ohio 43015.

Thomas, Jacques. *Magie du Boomerang*. Lyon, France: L'imprimerie des Beaux-Arts, 1985. Ambitious, large-format, 233-page study by a former air force helicopter pilot who became the father of boomeranging in his native France. Well-illustrated, with a wide, interesting range of photos.

——, ed., Boomerang-Club de France newsletter, 38 rue Madame, 75006, Paris, France.

Turck, A. *Théorie, Fabrication et Lancement des Boomerangs*. Paris, France: Editions Chiron, 1952. A study of killer-sticks as well as boomerangs. Extensively illustrated.

Urban, Willi. *Gehimnisvoller Bumerang*. Leutershausen, West Germany: 1966.

Veit, Gunther. *Bumerangs: Werfen, Fangen und Selberbauen*. Munich, West Germany: Hugendubel, 1983. A big, handsome book by the organizer of the German boomerang federation. Contains fine action photos.

——, ed. Deutscher Bumerang Club newsletter, Bruckenstrasse 24, 5500 Trier, West Germany.

Walker, Jearl. "The Amateur Scientist," *Scientific American*, March and April 1979. Two articles offering perhaps more than you want to know on the phenomenon of boomerang flight, by a Cleveland State physics professor who is a well-known science lecturer and author.

Weber, Klaus. *Der Bumerang—Ein Rotationsflugkorper*. Frankfurt, West Germany: ALS-Verlag, 1977.

# IV. WHERE TO SEE OLD BOOMERANGS

In the United States, there are major collections of boomerangs and related objects at the Museum of Natural History in New York City and at the Field Museum in Chicago. The Smithsonian Institution in Washington, D.C., has two collections: one is ethnographic and is held by the National Museum of Natural History; the other, focusing on aerodynamics and located in the National Air and Space Museum, was begun by turn-of-the-century flight theorist Samuel Langley and has been updated to include finely crafted contemporary specimens of boomerangs from around the world (including some that were used to set world competition records). The Museum of Flight in Seattle, Carnegie-Mellon Museum in Pittsburgh and the Science Museum in Buffalo, New York, are among other repositories with interesting collections.

There are treasure troves in some English museums, notably the British Museum in London, Cambridge University's museum and the Ashmoleon at Oxford University, where the wonderful Howard Carter finds from the tomb of King Tut in Egypt are held. On the continent, there are excellent collections in Paris, Florence, Leiden, Hanover and Vienna .

Australia, of course, is the mother lode. The South Australian Museum in Adelaide has some 5,000 specimens, including dozens of "prestige" boomerangs up to 10 feet long from the Cooper's Creek area. Another treasure is a single Twentieth Dynasty tomb throw-stick from Egypt, so valuable and fragile that it has never been thrown (despite the curator's temptation to try it out to see if it flies). There are good collections in the National Museum of Victoria in Melbourne, the Australian Museum in Sydney, the Western Australian Museum in Perth and the Queensland Museum in Brisbane.

# ABOUT THE AUTHORS

Co-author Benjamin Ruhe has been the primary force behind the recent interest in boomerangs in the United States. As honorary consultant in boomerangs to the Smithsonian's National Air and Space Museum, he organized thirteen annual boomerang festivals in Washington, D.C. and was one of the founders of the United States Boomerang Association. Having captained the U.S. team that successfully challenged Australia in 1981, he went on to lead the U.S. contingent that took top honors in the World Master's Cup in France in 1985. In 1977 he wrote the book *Many Happy Returns* (published in paperback as *Boomerang*), and today runs a thriving boomerang mail-order business out of Washington, D.C.

Inventor and designer Eric Darnell, ranked number two among international competitors, is author of the technical information presented in this book. He designed the world's first polypropylene boomerang, and the production-mold "Darnell," embodying his philosophy of producing safe, accurate and durable 'rangs, is the culmination of 28 years of boomerang-making experience. Incorporated in this book are such successful Darnell design experiments as hollowed undersides to improve hovering properties, wings of unequal length to reduce spin on return, bulbous tips for safer catches, undercut wingtips to increase flight time for MTA 'rangs, wind foilers, and a systematic method of tuning and weighting to deal with all sorts of throwing conditions. He has led the way in other innovative designs including "ambidextrous" boomerangs as well as 'rangs for distance throwing (dingle hook) and Fast-Catch. He was the first to conceive the idea of night-rangs, boomerangs lit with glowing cold-light chemicals.